PRAISE F
LIFE BLOWS UP

This wasn't the book I expected...it was better! As a journalist who followed with disgust the unfair character assassination that so completely altered the lives of two of the best people and finest public servants I know, I was looking for Cylvia Hayes to hit back hard at her media detractors for their distortions and cruelty. Instead, I found a book filled with forgiveness and love, and a story of rebirth and transformation that recognizes our deepest fears and hurt, and offers a path to healing. Instead of being consumed by rage, Cylvia Hayes was transformed by her "dark night of the soul" into a voice for reconciliation and renewal. I always respected her mind and courage; now I understand that her heart is even bigger. A fine read in our polarized times.

> —*John de Graaf, co-author of AFFLUENZA*
> *and co-founder of the Happiness Alliance*

When Life Blows Up is a living testimony to the power of forgiveness and the healing available when we allow Wholly Spirit to guide our lives. The book begins with the unasked for demolition of the life Cylvia Hayes knew and all the emotions that accompanied that. This beautiful book takes the reader on an intimate, vulnerable journey through her metamorphosis. All along the way, Hayes keeps the reader in mind, offering practical exercises to help someone who is going through their own disintegration and reinvention process. We witness forgiveness, and her spiritual practice, creating incremental shifts in her awareness and leading her to possibilities she never could have imagined. As she finds a new place in the world, we are given the hope that our place exists too. I loved the way Hayes wove her newly understood Christian upbringing and *Course in Miracles* consciousness into her story. The acknowledgement of the role ego played in her demise and her explanation of ego juxtaposed with True Self is honest and helpful. As she described disappearing through the steam from the hot tub into a world of presence and stillness, she transmits a sense of the light that is there for all of us. I think many readers will be in turn relating, wondering, and hopeful. If you have ever been, or are currently, in a crucible as intense as what Cylvia Hayes has experienced, I think you will find this a valuable read.

—*Rev. Jane Hiatt*
Senior Minister
Unity Community of Central Oregon

When Life Blows Up is at once a cautionary tale and a courageous self-examination from a woman who endured an insidious and devastating public shaming. Cylvia Hayes emerged from years of torment with a universal and eternal message for us all: as hard as it is, you must find a way to forgive those who trespassed against you. She has risen triumphantly and compassionately from childhood trauma, self-inflicted wounds, and a political scandal that wasn't. The "sweeping investigation" of Ms. Hayes and former Oregon Gov. John Kitzhaber trumpeted by Portland media turned up no criminal wrongdoing, leading hundreds of thousands of Oregonians to wonder, "In a free society, whose job is it to watch the watchdogs?"

—*Michael Davis, former executive editor of the Salem (OR) Statesman Journal*

I have known Cylvia Hayes for almost two decades and yet, after watching her struggle, sometimes despair, and finally overcome years of intense public criticism by filling her heart with love and forgiveness, I realize that I did not really know her at all. The courage required not only to undertake such a deeply honest self-evaluation of her own ego, but then to beautifully embrace and grow from the lessons learned is a testament to the power of the human spirit. This book can serve as an inspiration for anyone who feels that they can't possibly get up after life has knocked them down.

—*John Kitzhaber, former Oregon Governor*

When *Life* BLOWS UP

A Guide to Peace, Power and Reinvention

by

Cylvia Hayes

Columbus, Ohio

When Life Blows Up: A Guide to Peace, Power and Reinvention

Published by Gatekeeper Press
2167 Stringtown Rd, Suite 109
Columbus, OH 43123-2989
www.GatekeeperPress.com

ISBN (paperback): 9781642379082
eISBN: 9781642379099

CONTENTS

INTRODUCTION

Oh God. No, No, No!

S ometimes our lives just blow up. In one split second we know nothing is ever going to be the same again, and the way ahead looks really dark. My moment came October 7, 2014.

That day a caller informed me that a reporter had dug up some long-buried incidents from my past. He'd discovered that many years earlier, during the same period I'd been involved in a planned (at the time, illegal) marijuana-growing operation, I'd participated in a green card marriage for money.

This call wouldn't have been so terrifying if I hadn't been the life partner and fiancée to the governor of Oregon, who was running for reelection. In other words, I was Oregon's First Lady.

I had made the terrible mistake of getting into a high-profile public position without being totally honest about my past. When the story dropped, the media went wild, not just in my home state but across the country. Eventually, I even wound up in the inglorious pages of the UK tabloids.

Overnight, I became clickbait and the most humiliated person in the circles I'd been running in.

Some media and political opponents used the incidents from my past to launch a campaign of allegations that Governor John Kitzhaber and I had committed corruption and used our public positions for personal gains. Over time, this ordeal included being intensely investigated by the FBI, IRS, and U.S. Department of Justice; prolonged and unprecedented legal battles with the state's largest media institution; and an extreme smear campaign they kept up as a result.

My mistakes shredded the life of the person I loved most in the world, took a terrible toll on our family, destroyed my business, and created a lot of damage across state government as the governor's office and numerous agencies were buried under public records media requests and uncertainty about leadership and directives.

The enormity of it was surreal—it seemed so much bigger than I was. When I finally realized that it was going to take not months, but years to move through it, for the investigations to conclude, for my work to pick up again, it buckled my knees. *Who was I if I wasn't a successful social activist? Or a business owner? Or even someone people liked?*

In my lowest moments I would find myself wondering if maybe it was all true after all. Maybe I really was the ugly, valueless caricature being put forward in the media. I would physically flinch when my mind started down that path.

I didn't realize it at the time, but my whole life up until that point, I had doubted my own worth. Therefore, I craved validation from others. I came across as confident, but underneath was deep self-doubt which I masked by accomplishing things—in sports, through my work, and by being in leadership and public positions. Over the years I'd received quite a few accolades from others and I unconsciously used that to push the inner insecurity into a back corner of my mind. And then, in that moment, in the blink of an eye, everywhere I looked I was being invalidated. It wasn't just news headlines:

- ☞ My career, that seemed so central to my identity and sense of worth, was gone
- ☞ Ninety percent of the people I'd considered friends and colleagues vanished
- ☞ My beautiful, loving ten-year relationship with John was fractured.

What was left? Who was I?

In a sort of torturous irony, one of the things that helped me hold onto some sense of being more than just the valueless person being put forward in the media was that so much of the information was blatantly inaccurate. Yet, at the same time, the powerlessness to correct the misinformation and stop the escalating destruction of my reputation left me in despair and rage. Although I was in what looked like a position of power, I had never felt so powerless in my life.

The two most egregious sources of false information were the state's largest newspaper, the *Oregonian,* and its rival, the Portland-based *Willamette Week.* Over time, my attorneys and I documented dozens and dozens of examples of misinformation, enough to fill a volume in and of itself, but that is not the point of this book. A few of the most damaging examples help paint a picture of the media firestorm I found myself in.

The story that kicked off the campaign of false allegations appeared in the *Willamette Week* on October 8, 2014, and included more than a half dozen individual instances of false reporting. Some were just sloppy and relatively harmless like, "In the story she often tells, her mother fled Oklahoma after leaving Hayes' father." This was just bad reporting as I'd been on record many times saying my mother left Oklahoma with my father and I'd never said anything different. Other falsities were much more damaging to my reputation and legal battles were to follow.

One of the most harmful false claims was the one that said I had made more money after John got elected than before. The documented truth was that I had taken a significant reduction in income to step into public service but, despite providing the press with documentation of my income, that misreporting was never corrected.

The *Willamette Week* already had the information about the green card marriage when it published the first story accusing me of misusing my public position. In a strategic one-two punch, about twelve hours later the paper dropped the blast from my past piece and the media exploded.

Not wanting to be left behind, on October 13, 2014, the *Oregonian* ran an article claiming one of my clients had hired me because it wanted to pass specific state legislation. The client was a nonprofit, public education organization that had no legislative interest in or plan for Oregon.

The *Willamette Week* then claimed I ran my business out of Mahonia Hall, the governor's residence. It wasn't true. I lived only part-time at Mahonia Hall and my social enterprise consulting business, 3EStrategies, had always been registered out of Bend, Oregon, halfway across the state, where I actually lived.

The *Oregonian* ran a piece claiming the governor had only opposed coal export terminals because I had influenced him to do so to appease one of my clients. This, too, was false. I had no client that was paying me to work on the coal exports issue, and I had consistently opposed coal exports up to that point as a private citizen and professional clean energy advocate. The governor had his own long, storied history of environmental protection and support of transitioning to renewable energy that predated our relationship. The governor's communication director told us he had explained all this to the *Oregonian* reporter, who said he knew it was a "bogus, baseless" story, but if he didn't run it, *Willamette Week* would.

The competitive relationship between these two media outlets went back many years and was only exacerbated with the switch to a click-driven business model. The owner of the *Oregonian*, Advance Publications, run by billionaire brothers Donald and S.I. Newhouse, had been one of the first media firms in the United States to switch to the click-for-cash model which emphasized driving readers to the online version rather than the hard-copy newspaper and setting click quotas for reporters. Whether a reporter kept his or her job or earned bonuses was largely determined by the number of online clicks his or her stories generated. This naturally bred misinformation and sensationalism and Advance Publications was criticized for this erosion of sound, unbiased journalism by other media including the *New York Times* and *Columbia Journalism Review*.

Once one media outlet ran a story, most of the rest jumped to pass it on without fact-checking and the misinformation then spread like a virus. The way defamation laws are currently written, a person who is deemed a "public figure"—a very loosely defined term—has very little leverage to force the correction of media misinformation or pursue a defamation claim.

Over the next many months I would be stunned by the power the media has both in law and in the court of public opinion. I simply could not believe the intensity of the coverage. I was the front page of virtually every paper and the lead story in the television and radio news in Oregon and across the Pacific Northwest for weeks. Each day I would wake terrified to see what was being said about me.

The actual news outlets were one thing; their anonymous online commenters were something else again. I was called a tramp, Oregon's First Slut, a shack-up honey, a gold-digger, a shyster, and more. The viciousness and vileness shocked my psyche.

The violation that hurt the most, more than the lies and anonymous threats, was how my personal information was handled. Under public records laws, any of my emails dealing with business related to the State of Oregon had to be handed over to the media. I was fine with that. Any email I'd ever had with any state employee was stored on the state server and the state would supply those. The problem was that since I'd never been given a state email address or computer to use, my entire personal computer and all my emails had to be screened to see which were actually public records. This was an enormously invasive process. First, a tech team of people I didn't even know did a search of all my personal emails using a wide range of possible state-related words and phrases. They made a carbon copy of my entire computer hard drive—all photos, letters, and documents included. Then my attorneys looked through all of the emails and some of the documents. After that, a judge was appointed to review those emails and decide which were state-related business and which were personal. I hit a minor low point when one of the paralegals told me no matter how well they screened, they still came across some very personal correspondence between John and me.

In the end, well over one hundred thousand of my emails were released; the media went wild yet again. Shockingly, the *Oregonian* posted the bulk of the emails online and offered a "watchdog award" for any member of the public who could find some dirt in them. They didn't ask readers to find anything of importance, positive or negative, only negative. All they wanted was dirt, but nobody found any. There wasn't any to find.

Journalist and author John de Graaf, a friend and colleague of mine, posted:

> *This is one of the most disgusting examples of journalism I've ever seen.*
>
> *They make 94,000 emails, many of them personal, available to everybody, with no sense of personal privacy at all, then ask people to dig through them and point out the worst, most damaging ones, in order to win a "Watchdog" prize. I'm happy for people to see my email exchanges with*

Cylvia Hayes because they make clear her idealism and her efforts to help change society for the better, reducing inequality, protecting the environment, clean energy. I suspect that a truly thorough look at these, not a hatchet job, would reveal far more good intent than any alleged ... This makes me totally sick. I am ashamed for my profession as a journalist and for this complete corruption of the Fifth Estate.

But the supportive pushback was utterly drowned out by the frenzied mob. Not only by the thousands of nasty online comments to each media story, but also by the flow of crank phone calls and nasty, threatening emails—nearly all completely anonymous. The phone calls all came from men. One said, "Hi, sweetie. It sure is fun looking through the dirty underwear of your emails." Another, "My, you have been busy. Sluts usually are." Another, "Well, you gold-digging little tramp, how does it feel being spread open for the public?" And on and on it went.

The *Oregonian* and *Willamette Week* were creating something of a Samson and Delilah narrative, painting me as a corrupt, manipulative woman who was responsible for leading astray a strong, but love-blinded man. The Oregonian ran a Sunday cover story titled, *Kitzhaber's Final Days: the Inside Story of Ambition, Love, and Loyalty.* The entire piece was editorialized rather than hard fact and used only unnamed sources. It lied, claiming that before John got elected, I had been "struggling to generate a living from her green energy consulting business." In truth I had made far more money in the few years leading up to John's decision to run for governor again than at any point in my life. The so-called reporter called me a "flower-child-turned-green wonk" and "the one person whose naked self-interest and disregard for ethical boundaries led to his [Kitzhaber's] undoing." It was painful, to be sure. And it was unsettling because, even though the piece was editorial rather than factual, it was clear that someone from our inner circle was talking to the reporters and clearly willing to throw me under the bus.

While this was taking place, my attorneys were going through volumes and volumes of my personal journals. I wanted to proactively give the investigators every bit of legal and business information they asked for because I knew I hadn't committed corruption or influence-peddling. However, my personal journals were *personal*! They included my feelings about relationships, my personal struggles, etc. It was violation enough that my attorneys would be looking through them, but then someone suggested we have an intern scan every page so that we could do searches for specific terms. At this point I had no faith that anything could be kept private and I flatly refused to have my journals scanned.

As the frenzy built, anonymous death and rape threats started coming in and I picked up a couple of prolific postal stalkers who would send notes pieced together with letters and pictures cut from magazines and newspapers. These usually including some unflattering mocked-up photos of me and were often carefully decorated and even trimmed with pinking shears. To think of strangers spending hours obsessing over me was deeply disturbing. The whole experience was a psychic gut punch; I simply couldn't believe there were so many people who hated me and wished me harm.

In an effort to prevent John from losing the election, the governor's staff and campaign team tried to minimize coverage of the allegations. Any public utterance I made just added to the media frenzy, so we adopted a strategy that no matter what the media printed or aired, I would not respond. This was very hard to stomach as I desperately wanted to defend myself. In retrospect, I believe it was a mistake. Looking back, I would have handled the media much differently. I would not have bent over backwards to try to give them documentation and I would have pushed back hard against all the misinformation, calling out the egregious inaccuracies from the beginning. By not doing so, we let the media and political opponents take complete control of the narrative and let the trial-by-media run unchallenged.

The feeding frenzy rolled forward and John's political opponents, including jealous rivals in his own party, sensing blood in the water, did nothing to step up in support. Some even jumped into the fray. Nearly all of my colleagues also stayed silent—much later, many would sheepishly confess they'd been afraid of saying anything for fear the *Oregonian* or *Willamette Week* would come after them.

I had become the chink in the seemingly impenetrable armor of Governor Kitzhaber's long-standing political dominance—I was chum in the water. The humiliation and powerlessness tore at me like a wild, sharp-fanged beast. I had never had so many people know of my existence, yet also had never felt so utterly alone. The barrage of hatred, ill will, and animosity was deeply shocking and left me questioning if anything I'd ever believed about myself or anyone else was really true.

The emotional tsunami triggered flashbacks to deep traumas I had suffered in my childhood, when beloved and trusted adults violated my body, my dignity, and my sense of safety. The new savagery tore open old wounds I'd thought had healed.

While the legal and media attacks dragged on and on, John and I were dealing with the tremendous grief of having lost our work and reputations, suffering serious financial challenges due to the loss of income and my business, and all the associated legal fees. His son was in a terrible head-on car crash. John was in a separate car crash. In a horse-riding incident, I broke my leg nearly off just above the ankle. All of it was covered in the media. Often, I felt utterly powerless, just watching as my life and dreams turned to dust and slithered through my fingers.

Finally, after two and a half years of intensive and invasive investigation, the federal agents determined there were no grounds for filing charges and dropped the case. But that didn't stop the media attacks or legal challenges. The Oregon Government Ethics Commission kicked off a separate investigation and the *Oregonian* demanded I pay for its attorneys' fees for going through my emails, to the tune of approximately $130,000. Eventually, in what has been reported as an unprecedented move in the history of media and politics in the United States, the *Oregonian* put a lien on my house even though I was actively appealing the claim. I filed for bankruptcy to protect my home.

This long, excruciating ordeal completely changed my life. Fortunately, unbelievably, and blessedly, it changed it in ways I never could have imagined.

This book is not the one I set out to write. I first started working on it a few months into the horrific events. Those early drafts detail the vast amount of media misinformation and Machiavellian political betrayals. At that point, in my rage and pain, those were the stories I wanted to tell. I wanted to say, "Look, those were lies. I'm not the ugly, corrupt person the attackers painted me to be." But that was when I was still allowing the opinions of others to shape my opinion of myself. I now realize it was before I really knew my True Self at all. I got the chance to begin to meet her through the long and brutal journey of having the identity I'd worked so hard to create ripped to pieces.

In the passage through my big ordeal, I took a deep dive into research and experimentation with reinvention, resiliency, and this crafty thing we call ego. I'm not talking about ego in the sense that modern pop culture defines it but rather as the ancient Greeks viewed it, as something of a construct we create; a false set of beliefs about ourselves. The ego is the personality we build over time; the root of the word 'personality' is from the Latin *persona*, which originally referred to the mask an actor donned as he stepped on stage to play a role. On a spiritual level, ego is that part of ourselves that feels small, separate, and alone. It's the mask we hide behind, believing it is protecting us when in fact, it is keeping us from the awesome truth of who we really are.

It took three years for me to understand that the events that broke my life aren't what matter; what matters is what broke open as a result. Life as I knew it was so completely upended, for such a prolonged period of time, that I had to learn new survival skills. I could not force my way through the world anymore. With my psyche on the verge of cracking, I turned inward to a journey that would, over time, reveal diamonds rather than demons. I learned the art of separating my inner state of being, my peace and happiness, from the circumstances swirling through my life. I gained greater patience, which had always been a challenge, and learned to better trust divine timing. I learned to intentionally choose my feelings—that's right, we *do* actually have a choice in what and how we feel. I moved through the terribly difficult process of forgiving those who had orchestrated the attacks, and even more difficult, forgiving myself.

So I share these stories and experiences to offer encouragement. Sometimes terrible things happen to us. Sometimes we make terrible mistakes. Life shatters, and all our believed and beloved certainties are stripped away. We face loss, betrayal, or assault, or we simply reach a certain age and find we aren't where we thought we'd be and aren't sure where to go next.

This book is for all of us whose lives have blown up, who have been sent hurtling off in directions we would never have chosen, and who, facing the unthinkable and the catastrophic, are determined to thrive on the other side.

We are living in a time of extraordinary and rapid change both in our world and our personal lives. Many of us are facing the reinvention of careers, relationships, identities, and selves at a time we never thought we'd need to. Asked for or not, believe it or not, this presents a huge opportunity because growth, success, and progress don't happen without change. The key is learning how to find peace and power in the midst of change so that we can heal, make purpose of the pain, and direct the change toward making a better life.

The field of uncertainty, though challenging, is a place of immense power. Getting rattled and displaced gives us a chance to build a stronger foundation for launching anew. Being whittled down makes space for our True Selves to emerge. Our shaken moments can open beautiful portals into an awesome adventure of self-revelation, reinvention, and love. In the seeming destruction lies the golden opportunity not to break down, but to break through and break open.

We might not have asked for what's happening, and it might not be our fault, but no matter what, it *is* our responsibility because, while circumstances may be out of our control, how we handle them is not. I don't know if everything happens for a purpose, but I do know we can find purpose in everything that happens. Choosing to *grow* through the ordeal, rather than just go through it, is one of our most empowering decisions.

Over the past four years I've explored, taken courses, and reached out to all sorts of teachers and therapists. I've studied the mental and emotional habits of people who are making big contributions but also seem to be living peaceful, dialed-in lives. All of that was well and good and useful and I learned a lot, but the real power was the mind-blowing direct experience of what was happening in my inner life during the train wreck that was my outer life. I learned that surviving, overcoming, and thriving isn't so much about analyzing and gathering information as it is about remembering who we really are to begin with; it's about coming home.

The concepts, experiences, and insights put forward here are grounded in neuroscience, psychology, numerous spiritual traditions, and practical metaphysics. They come from the understanding that we are spiritual beings having a human experience and that we are more, much more, than these bodies we wear.

My goal with this book is to offer some helpful tools and insights to anyone in the process of reinventing careers, relationships, and their very lives and identities. It's especially for those who are facing such reinvention in the aftermath of catastrophic life challenges and losses. My hope is that it helps heal hearts and minds that are reeling, reinventing, and, most importantly, evolving.

I share some very personal stories and key insights and strategies that helped me survive my own traumatic upheaval, hit the restart button, and thrive on the other side. My prayer is that this helps readers remember we already have everything we need inside ourselves to:

☞ Calm fear in the face of crisis
☞ Get a grip on our racing, spinning, anxiety-riddled minds
☞ Manage loss of control and embrace the power of surrender
☞ Take back our power
☞ Find forgiveness, even of self, in the midst of loss and costly mistakes
☞ Develop a sense of genuine self-worth and safety
☞ Embrace the more that we are.

I had faced some serious hardship in my life but nothing could have prepared me for the epic, uncomfortable, messy, and indescribably beautiful odyssey of meeting my True Self. I hope this book helps ease others who are on a similar journey.

Part One

Surviving the Blast

CHAPTER 1

Fear

"Fear defeats more people than any other one thing in the world."

—*Ralph Waldo Emerson*

Life has countless ways to hit us hard, knock us off-balance, and rock our very foundations. The loss of the job we'd poured ourselves into and believed to be secure. A business failure. The death of a loved one. A cancer diagnosis. Your spouse doesn't want to be married anymore. Your partner's sleeping with someone else. You reach a certain point in your life and nothing looks like you thought it would.

One constant boiling through nearly every truly seismic life event is fear.

As the public shaming and political assault roared forward with hurricane velocity, fear was everywhere and ever-present.

The governor's staff was panicked; the campaign staff was panicked. We decided I should do a press conference to address the incidents from my past.

During a mostly sleepless night I wrote the bulk of what would become my statement. The following morning I, the governor's chief of staff and his communications team, and later, my attorney, met at the campaign office. We alerted the press that I would hold a press conference at 4 p.m. I was running on fear, fumes, and adrenaline, with stress levels so high I felt like I was going to pass out.

At the World Trade Center in downtown Portland, we walked past a throng of milling reporters and went into a green room where the staff could fire questions at me. *How much did you get paid for the illegal marriage? What did you use the money for? Did you tell Governor Kitzhaber about it? When did you move to Oregon?* Finally, one asked, *"Why isn't the governor here?"* and it stopped me in my tracks, or rather in my heart.

Tearfully, I said, "Because I feel so bad about what this is doing to him that I can't look at him and talk about it without crying." The room was totally silent and the staff person who'd asked the question had tears rolling down her cheeks. I thought I might throw up again.

Finally, they led me out of the green room, through the pack of reporters, and to the podium. Cameras clicked, flashbulbs popped. I prayed I would be able to keep my voice from shaking and not break down sobbing. I faced the press, took a few deep breaths, and through tears and hand-shaking stress said the following:

> *Seventeen years ago I made a serious mistake*
> *by committing an illegal act when I married*

a person so that he could retain residency in the United States. It was a marriage of convenience. He needed help and I needed financial support.

We were both living in Washington. I was attending Evergreen State College, and we were introduced by mutual acquaintances. This was a difficult and unstable period in my life. I want to be clear today: I was associating with the wrong people. I was struggling to put myself through college and was offered money in exchange for marrying a young person who had a chance to get a college degree himself if he were able to remain in the United States.

We met only a handful of times. We never lived together. I have not had any contact with him since the divorce finalized in 2002.

It was wrong then, and it is wrong now, and I am here today to accept the consequences, some of which will be life-changing. And I cannot predict what direction this will go.

In the few years after this bad decision, I completed my degree, got my feet underneath me, and established my home and career in Oregon. I became an active and engaged civic volunteer, community member, and I became active politically.

My decision to marry illegally felt very, very distant and far removed from the life I was building. I was ashamed and embarrassed.

Therefore I did not share this information even with John once we met and started dating.

This is the most painful part for me. John Kitzhaber deserved to know the history of the person he was forming a relationship with. The fact that I did not disclose this to him meant that he has learned about this in the most public and unpleasant way. This is my greatest sorrow in this difficult situation.

I apologize deeply for my actions and omissions, first and foremost to John, the person I love and respect above all others. I also apologize to my friends, family, and colleagues who have trusted and supported me. And to Oregonians, I deeply regret not being right up front about the fact that I had made a serious mistake. I owe you all an apology.

The work that I do on behalf of our environment and trying to make people's lives better is incredibly important to me— it's the focal point of my life. I will continue to do my best in that arena going forward. But for the time being, there are more important issues. I need to take some personal time to reflect and address this difficult situation and to focus on my relationship with John.

The press corps seemed almost stunned for a moment, silent, then they pelted me with questions. I answered them all directly until eventually I was ushered out a back door behind the podium, into an elevator, and to a vehicle. I was so stressed and shell-shocked that to this day I have no memory of the elevator moving, getting out, the car that I was put into, or who was driving.

The details of all of this and more, some true and some not, would spill out across the state and national media over several weeks as we moved toward the election on November 4, 2014. It would become a media feeding frenzy the likes of which Oregon politics had never seen before.

John was under tremendous pressure, and even the attorneys were paranoid. One of them, I don't remember who, suggested the feds might raid my home at any time. *What? My God!* How could this be happening?

I was constantly, acutely stressed, terrified, sleeping poorly, mind racing, stomach churning, and nauseous. Most of us have had the experience of having a terrible dream, then waking with a wave of relief when we realize it wasn't actually happening, but was just a nightmare. Well, during that period of my life I longed for such an experience because every day I would wake up, begin to remember what was going on, and feel like I was waking *into* a nightmare, dawn blinking back into darkness.

- ☞ What was the latest news story saying?
- ☞ Would there be another death or rape threat?
- ☞ What was going to happen with my work?
- ☞ How could I survive this financially?
- ☞ Was the person I loved most in the world going to leave me?
- ☞ Was he going to recover?

I was in full "fight-my-attacker" mode, highly adrenalized, extremely stressed, my nerves so frayed I jumped at things I'd see moving in my peripheral vision. Even my sweat smelled different, ranker than usual. The fear was so extreme it was a tangible entity, a force, a beast.

Experiencing truly life-altering change—a catastrophic injury, loss of income, the end of a foundational relationship—can trigger the primal feeling of being threatened, in danger of actual, physical harm or destruction. Fear is one of the most powerful emotions we experience, and literally, physically changes the chemistry of our bodies and alters our behavior.

We have the ability to experience fear for good reason. It developed in our species as a survival mechanism when we had to rely on our fight-or-flight instincts and quick physical responses to stay out of the clutches of sharp-fanged predators and it is still invaluable in instances where we have to react to avoid getting hit by a car or, in really unfortunate cases, getting hit by another human being. It's also useful in getting us to think twice before diving off a bridge, climbing onto a wild bronco, or dashing in front of a fast-moving train.

However, fear is not useful in dealing with things that don't require a quick physical response, things like what another person is going to say about us, whether we're going to have enough money to pay the bills, or if the cancer remission is going to last. When facing those types of situations, being consumed by fear will only make things worse by undermining our health, driving us toward depression, prompting us to make poor choices. Fear also paralyzes us from moving toward the things we do want.

During periods of acute change, fear in and of itself can add to the trauma. It is certainly responsible for sending a lot of stress hormones rampaging through our bodies, eroding our sleep, and gnawing away our peace; fear nearly always makes the mess in front of us appear much bigger than it really is.

Up to that point in my life, I'd say I'd been pretty courageous. I had raced horses, ridden bulls (well, one smallish bull, once), become the first female heavy equipment operator in King County Washington, and was a first-generation college graduate. I'd survived violent assault and had run for political office. None of it took the toll of having my life spin out of control at the age of forty-seven, being at the mercy of media and federal investigators, sitting in uncertain and intense circumstances with no perceived ability to control the outcome, and facing the fact that it was going to go on for years and involve dozens of attorneys and officials and the media.

There was no move I could make, no action to take, to force the fearful thing to go away. It was not a situation I could tackle head-on and resolve, or something I could undo or let die and move on from. In previous hardships I had always been able to fight my way through, work harder, buckle down, or cut loose unhealthy relationships, but none of that was going to work with what I had before me. I could no longer rely on being able to force things through in the circumstances of my life.

And so, I got the unasked for *opportunity* to really sit with and examine fear with an objectivity I had never employed before. I came to see that even though the fear was so intense it felt like I was being physically threatened, in truth my survival just then was not dependent upon fighting off attackers, but upon managing stress and maintaining mental health in the midst of extremely difficult circumstances. I had to find a way to take my mind back from the ping-ponging, frantic antics of fear in order to be able to function. My sanity, and possibly my literal survival, depended upon finding something I hadn't known existed; a way to disconnect my inner state of being from the events swirling through my life. I had to be able to find some semblance of peace and inner calm while sitting directly in the middle of a giant and terrifying mess I couldn't control. This took me on a journey that turned out to be one of the best gifts I never imagined.

The first major help came while reading Eckhart Tolle's *The Power of Now*. Prior to the big crisis I had meditated regularly for years, and I believe it may have saved my life when everything blew to pieces. However, I had never taken the meditation beyond the short periods assigned to it. In fact, I had a sort of Type-A meditation practice. I'd wake up, bang out my meditation, cross it off the to-do list, and then launch into the rest of the busy, and honestly, far from meditative day. What I learned from Tolle's work was the concept of taking the meditative mindset beyond the practice mat by coming into the present moment, over and over and over again, throughout the course of each day.

I began to learn the life-changing art of presencing. Each time I'd get spun up in fear, mind racing, stomach clenching, I'd bring my awareness back to the very moment I was in. I would take a breath and ask myself, *"Am I under attack right now? Is that reporter actually going to bust down my front door? Is the mortgage company trying to foreclose on my house? Do I know for sure my business will never amount to anything again?"*

The answer was always no, and I could then recapture my mind and recognize that the fear consuming me was actually about things that weren't happening at that moment and might not ever happen. I could recognize that I was eating myself alive with fear over future *imagined* possibilities and freaking out over things that might not ever even happen!

This was a deeply empowering realization. We spend so much of our lives in fear of dreaded imagined future outcomes that never come to pass. I never even saw the heavy hits coming—the blown knee, my sister's death, the public character assassination. They just hit out of the blue. I can't remember one single thing that I fearfully obsessed about that actually turned out the way I feared it would. What a waste of time and mind and peace! As Mark Twain once observed, "I am an old man and have known many troubles. Most of them never happened."

On June 16, 2017, two years and eight months after it all began, I was standing in line at the local community grocery store buying eggs when my cell phone exploded. Friends were sending texts; my PR rep was calling. A Google alert with my name flashed and I clicked the link. I must have gasped because both the checker and the woman in front of me in line looked over and asked if I was okay. I said, "I think my life is blowing up, but this time in a good way." On the screen in my hand was the announcement that all the federal investigations had been dropped, having found no grounds to file charges. We were exonerated of the false allegations.

I walked out toward the car where John had been waiting, finding him pacing back and forth in the parking lot, talking on his phone. Excitedly, I rushed up to him, waving to get his attention. He nodded excitedly and pointed to his phone, mouthing the name of his attorney. When he hung up, we just looked at each other, sort of stunned. One of us, I don't remember who, asked, "Is it really over?" We weren't completely sure. We had been planning to go to the gym right after the grocery store, but simultaneously we said some version of "Screw it, let's go get a beer!"

Through all of it, the feds had never raided my house, (In fact, throughout the whole ordeal I never even met them!) My career wasn't destroyed; seriously reshaped, but not destroyed. John and I are still together, and our family came out healthier than ever before. And, at least up until the date of this writing, not one person has ever been ugly to my face—all the nastiness has been anonymous or behind the protection of a computer screen or media institution.

Now don't get me wrong. I'm not saying making it through public shaming, or any other major life-blowing-up event, should feel like a cakewalk. Even after the federal investigation was dropped, it would be another two and a half years before all of the legal challenges and financial devastation from this event were finally behind me. During that time, in some ways the uncertainty and the financial challenges deepened, and managing fear was one of the greatest challenges.

Some of the fears did merit action and certain decisions. For example, paying attention to the very real financial concerns led me to be more creative and flexible in generating income and cutting costs than I might have been otherwise. Maintaining a pretty frugal approach simplified things when I reached the point of needing to file bankruptcy to protect my house from the *Oregonian*. And my ongoing worry about John likely kept me more open, loving, and vigilant in supporting him where I could. However, most of the dreaded imagined terrors that had chewed my mind and stolen sleep the first many horrific months of the ordeal never came to pass. Training myself to be aware of how much of my fear had been imagination-based proved to be one of the most effective survival strategies for coping with the many long months of challenges to follow.

I learned to take a step back and objectively examine the fear, to be able to decipher whether or not the various fears were due to actual threats. Most of them weren't, and each time I recognized that, I gained a greater ability to take back control of my mind.

One of the most important applications of my new approach to fear management had to do with navigating the greatest terror of all. I rarely voiced it, even to myself, because it was too terrible to face, but down deep, as months dragged into years and my career and income still hadn't rebounded and certain media interests continued to smear me, I would find myself wondering if perhaps my life really had been destroyed, perhaps the damage was too big to overcome. Each time I believed the legal challenges were just about over, only to be told the process had been extended a few more months. Each time I was rejected by a prospective client or employer, an evil little whisper would say, "*Maybe it is impossible for someone nearing fifty to really succeed on the other side of all of this."*

I learned to be able to face that demon and remind myself that I was only fearing potential, imagined outcomes and events that might never come to pass. I would bring my mind into the present moment and remind myself that I was, in that very moment, basically safe, alive, and even, for the most part, happy. The terror would ease, my breathing would resume, and life moved forward.

There is often an added layer of fear when facing major life upheaval and uncertainty at midlife and beyond. It can feel like there is less runway ahead, less room for correction and renewal. The truth is, however, added life experience and perspective have equipped us with abilities we didn't have earlier in our lives. Once we release the fear, this added life experience is a power that can be tapped to produce incredible feats of creativity and reinvention.

Fear is learned through the guidance of our parents and through our own falls and hurts and heartaches. Some of it we're hardwired for, like the fear of abandonment and isolation. Another layer is piled on from the culture of fear we're experiencing in our current media and political atmosphere. We're literally saturated with fear, which can compound the dread when something catastrophic happens in our personal lives, even to the point of becoming incapacitating.

Fear is programmed into us. With discipline, we can train ourselves to determine which fears merit action and which are just a waste of time, mind, energy, and peace. A thing learned can be unlearned. This particular unlearning is liberating beyond imagination. Eleanor Roosevelt famously said, "You gain strength, courage, and confidence by every experience in which you really stop to look fear in the face."

Strategies for Taming Fear

☞ Learn the art of "presencing," of practicing being in the Present Moment.

The simple fact is that unless we train ourselves differently, most of us spend the bulk of our lives focused on the past or the future, often in fear. If you're reading this book, you're likely dealing with some difficult, even traumatic situation right now. There are probably a lot of unknowns, worry, angst. But ask yourself this: right now, in *this very moment,* are you basically okay? Are you right now under direct attack? In this very moment are you warm? Do you have shelter and food? Are you breathing? If you have time to read this sentence, your answer is almost certainly yes!

To become present, look around you right now, wherever you are. Notice the sights. Take a deep breath through your nose and notice the scents. Listen to the many sounds and the little silences between them. Feel the chair beneath you, supporting you. Focus on the breath gently moving in and out of your body. Feel the rhythm of your beating heart. Run your right hand gently across the top of your left. Notice. Breathe. Say aloud, "*I Am here. I Am here. I Am here.*"

Let your body release its tensions—loosen your jaw. Drop your shoulders. Underneath all the noises and sounds, feel the deep stillness of the earth and sea. Breathe deeply. Look around and feel this moment in time. Release and relax.

Developing a presencing practice takes exactly that— practice. The more times each and every day you bring your focus back to the present moment, even for just a second or two, the calmer and less stressed you will be. Not only will this help you navigate trauma more easily, but it will add all sorts of additional beauty and richness to the good times.

Coming into the present moment gives you the space to clarify the fears that are about imagined future happenings, those that are about things you have no control over, and those that might actually merit some action. I highly recommend reading *The Power of Now*, by Eckert Tolle.

This very moment, this instant of *now*, is really the only thing we can control. The state of consciousness we choose in this moment sets the stage for what happens next. In the now we can choose the feeling we want to experience. That's right—you do not have to be at the mercy of your emotions. You have a choice in how you feel and you can learn to wield this power with skill and consistency, even when facing extraordinary challenges.

Finally, practicing being in the present moment is one aspect of meditation. In the early stages of my life blowing up I didn't have the tools I now have to keep centered and healthy in the storm. I did, however, have an established longstanding meditation practice which was just about the only thing that gave me the power to tame the fear and keep my panicked thoughts from overwhelming me. I talk more about meditation and the mind in later chapters.

☞   Do a fear versus reality exercise

Take a sheet of paper and draw a line down the middle to make two columns. Recall a time in your recent past when you were really fearful or worried about some potential event or outcome. When you felt frantic over some crisis. Let yourself really feel how the fear was affecting you, your thoughts, your body, your sleep patterns. In the left-hand column, write down this feared thing and the terrible outcomes you imagined or expected.

Now remember what actually happened and in the right-hand column write down what actually came to be. Did the feared event turn out as you imagined? Was it as bad as you feared? Where is that big challenge now? What was the damage done or the loss suffered? Did any positive growth or learning occur? Were there beautiful aspects of it that you didn't see coming?

Sometimes feared things do come to pass. The loved ones we worry about meet tragedy. Our unwise or misguided decision costs us our home or freedom. The person we want to be with leaves us. This human experience brings hardship, and sometimes we can see the hardship coming. However, most of the time we don't, and most of our modern-day fear is based on imagination and speculation about possible future events that may or may not shake out a certain way. These unmerited fears do nothing except rob us of our power, peace, and well-being.

Fear is a universal shared aspect of our human experience and traumatic change and loss, especially when we don't see it coming, is usually terrifying. Fear management is a critical skill in the blast zone. On the other side of the blast, once the rubble has been cleared, skillful fear management is an unbelievably powerful tool to shift from surviving to thriving. Once the extreme events have passed, the new reservoir of inner calm and ease benefits every facet of our lives, making the bumps a lot easier to glide over and the beauties deeper and more joy-filled.

I now know, from deeply personal experience, that it is possible to use what we learn in the crisis to rebuild. It may well be that all the king's horses and all the king's men can't put us back the way we were before, but as we gather up the broken pieces, we will have opportunities to put them back together so they are more beautiful, peace-filled, and powerful. Our resilience is part of our brilliance, and every single moment is a rebirth, whether we're conscious of it or not. Life doesn't happen in the future or the past; it happens in each present moment. And in each present moment, when we drop our attachment to the past and our fear of the future, we start anew.

CHAPTER 2

Treat the Trauma

"Don't despair if your heart has been through a lot of trauma. Sometimes that's how beautiful hearts are remade: they are shattered first."

—Yasmin Mogahed

I f we get hit by a car and break our leg, we get professional medical treatment. Getting hit by a major life blow is just as traumatic and worthy of professional healing support. The wound might not show on our bodies, but a bruised and wounded psyche is every bit as real as a shattered bone.

Early on in the media assault, when panic was the general backdrop, I rushed from the state capital to my home three hours away to collect all the documents the attorneys thought might be needed by the FBI and IRS investigators.

I arrived in a frantic state. The security officer parked in my narrow asphalt driveway, made lumpy by large roots from the towering pine tree in the front yard. I blasted into my small house, secured the cats in the spare bedroom so they couldn't go hide somewhere, and quickly started gathering my things. I was breathing shallowly, very jumpy, keeping all doors locked and an eye on windows. It sickened me that I now felt unsafe in the beloved little home that had been such a refuge over the past years.

I scrambled with boxes of records and documents, shoving them willy-nilly into my car in the cramped one-car garage. My heart was racing and I was damp with foul-smelling sweat and had to keep reminding myself to breathe and not just pant. Finally, I loaded the two cats into my fully packed Prius and pulled out of the garage. Normally the security driver would have followed me, but I was so stressed and jumpy that I wasn't even sure I could remember the route I'd driven dozens of times, so I asked him to lead and pulled my car in behind his as we headed back over the mountain.

Although relieved to be in my own car, driving myself, and to be alone, I was still extremely, nauseously nervous. My mind was wild, replaying over and over the many humiliations of the past ten days, racing forward trying to imagine what might happen next. I seethed with anger at the reporters who were profiting from publicly assassinating my character and spreading so much speculation and misinformation about John and me.

And then, suddenly, I was sobbing. Like a dam giving way, the pain broke through the anger in deep, raging torrents. The intensity seized me; the source surprised me. The

46

memories that were ripping sobs from my soul were not of the media attacks but from further back, to my childhood— Dad's abuse, Mom's breakdowns, my inability to protect her or my little brother. I couldn't believe that after all this time and all the work I'd done, those memories and old traumas were resurfacing. After all the counseling, reflecting, and soul-searching to heal those wounds, here they were, front and center once again. It pissed me off and left me in despair. Like bondage, heavy shackles were chaining those old, weary experiences to the trauma currently blowing up in my life. Utterly exhausted, the terrible thought that I'd never be able to escape the cycle, that somehow I was irreparably damaged, settled into a corner of my battered mind.

I would have pulled the car over and curled up on myself right then had it not been that the security officer I was following would have come back to check and found me in the fetal position. I would not let that happen, so I kept driving, sobbing, struggling to see through the tears.

Just as another round of sobbing tore loose, Lucy, the old, somewhat decrepit calico, stepped onto my lap and puked all over my leg. I wiped up the vomit with paper napkins from the console, trying to stay on the road, took a few more ragged breaths, calmed down, and kept driving. Lucy curled up in my lap and fell asleep. Nothing like a little gritty real life and smelly bodily fluids to bring a wandering, floundering mind back to the present moment.

Although frustrated and resentful, I knew I was in deep psychological and emotional trauma and made the decision to see a therapist about the terrible jumble of layered, distressing memories and horrifying current events. A dear and respected friend recommended a therapist who worked with Eye Movement Desensitization and Reprogramming (EMDR).

EMDR therapy is based on the premise that our brains process and cluster memories during REM sleep, when our eyes are moving back and forth in bilateral motion. During EMDR therapy, the client focuses on emotionally disturbing memories and thoughts while the therapist applies external bilateral stimuli such as directed eye movements or side-to-side tapping sounds.

I wasn't sure EMDR was scientifically valid, but I wasn't sure it wasn't either and I liked the fact that it was something I hadn't already tried. I had nothing to lose.

A week later I sat on a small couch in a quiet little office; the therapist sat in a chair opposite and to my left. She had given me a sheet of paper with a list of statements and asked me to identify the one that seemed to be most true about how I felt about myself. With little hesitation, I hit on, "*I am not good enough.*" Then, secondarily, I noted the statement, "*I am damaged beyond repair.*"

Next, she asked me to think of a specific time when I remembered not feeling good enough. My memories started with a couple of speaking engagements during which I had gotten really nervous. As I thought about those, the therapist played back-and-forth tapping sounds in my headset—left, right, left, right. *Tap, tap, tap, tap.* Memories skipped back to when I had won a statewide trophy for my 4-H speech. I was eight or nine and had won against eighteen-year-olds. I remembered being very nervous about that speech and then very proud when I won. In preparation for the speech, my father had drilled me and made me practice but he never showed up for the competition. For years afterwards, he took credit for my win, saying he'd won the trophy because of how he'd prepared me.

The tapping stopped and the therapist asked, "What are you feeling?"

"Really angry. Incredibly angry at my father," I said.

I put the headphones back on. A different memory popped up.

I was very young, maybe three or four, and my family had been watching *Born Free*, but apparently my parents had left to get ready for bed. I was watching the ending by myself and I was terribly upset and sad about the lady chasing the lioness away. I was sobbing, and my older brother came and scooped me up and took me into my parents' room. My dad scolded and berated me for crying, for being a "sissy little girl."

I told the therapist I didn't see how one memory led to another. She said both events were about being strong, having to step up and overcome emotions.

Surprisingly, that memory led to other memories of my older brother and sister. I flashed on an old, old memory—I was very young—of opening the door to my bedroom and gagging on fumes. My sister was lying on her back, spraying something into a washcloth on her face. My mother pushed past me, grabbed my sister by the hair, and yanked her off the bed. Years later I learned that my parents had forbidden her to leave the house and she had been trying to inhale aerosol deodorant in an effort to get high. My sister was so beautiful. She died at fifty of a drug overdose. I was flooded with a thick sadness and tenderness for the tragedy of my older brother and sister's lives.

After the session I felt drained and dazed. The therapist gave me a homework assignment to make a list of my most traumatic memories. Inwardly, I said, *"Oh shit. That's the last thing I want to do."* That night my sister walked my dreams.

A week later, as the media firestorm raged and anonymous hate mail flowed in, I headed to my second EMDR session. Just as I was pulling up to the building, I got an email from the reporter who had put the whole smear campaign into motion, informing me he was doing another article. My first reaction was, *"This fucker is just relentless."* My second was to wonder, for the hundredth time, why the man was so determined to harm me. I didn't understand it.

With that and a sense of dread, holding my timeline of traumas in hand, I walked into the therapist's office.

The intensity of that session and those that followed over the next several months are impossible to describe. I opened up about the old abuse—my mom hospitalized, the whippings, the molestation, all the screaming. The worst wasn't what had been done to me but what I had done—the beatings I'd inflicted on animals I dearly loved when rage overtook me. The suffocating, claustrophobic sense of being overwhelmed by the responsibility of trying to protect myself, my mom, my brother, the animals—sometimes even trying to protect them from myself.

Yes, it was a lot. Like so many of us, I'm sure I could write an entire book about my crazy, deeply dark, and yet stunningly beautiful childhood, but that wasn't what was important. I'm not suggesting we make light of the damage done by the traumas we suffer, especially as children; facing these experiences is a crucial step in healing, transforming, and releasing ourselves from their influence. However, the most important thing isn't the trauma we suffer but what we choose to do with it. That, and not the trauma itself, is what defines us.

I had grown a lot, and come a long way from the damage done in my childhood, but finally, amazingly, right there in the middle of my blown-to-pieces life, through the help of EMDR and a good therapist, I found freedom and began to rewrite my story. Painful memories lost their bite. I developed compassion for the little girl who had hurt those she loved because she was being hurt and didn't know how else to respond.

Sometimes treating fresh trauma brings healing to deep, old, festering wounds. Abrupt, intense pain can open cracks that let light pour into old, dark corners, scrubbing away stains, evaporating shadows, illuminating, empowering.

Strategies for Effective Approaches to Therapy

☞ During heavy trauma, the sooner you seek professional support, the better. If you don't treat a broken bone soon enough, it can heal malformed. Unprocessed traumatic events can do the same to our memories and emotions.

☞ One size does not fit all. EMDR worked for me, but it's just one of many, many different types of therapy. It's not for everyone. The important thing is to stay open and go with what feels right for you. Not only are there different types of therapy but there are a lot of different therapists. There's a possibility you might not land with the right therapist on the first try. Listen to yourself if it truly feels like the type of treatment you're getting isn't helping. If so, try a different therapist. *However*, don't blame the therapist for your discomfort in dealing with your trauma. The simple truth is most deeply valuable breakthrough therapy pushes us out of our comfort zones. But, if you're in a place where you're considering therapy, you might want to ask yourself just how comfortable your current comfort zone actually is.

☞ Do the homework assignments. A good therapist doesn't fix anything for you but rather guides you in fixing yourself. Be open. Be vulnerable. The homework is often more important than the actual session. Having done a good deal of personal healing and development work, and now as a professional coach, I can say for sure that with therapy, like so much of life, you'll get out of it what you put into it.

☞ Stay open to the possibility that the therapy will have massive, positive, unforeseen benefits. What have you got to lose by entertaining that outcome?

Navigating deep life trauma is a time to prioritize our self. Mental health therapy and personal development work have lost a lot of the stigma they used to hold, but there is still a prevalent tendency to treat it as a luxury, something that often can't be added to the already-full plate. But consider, when it all comes right down to it, the single most important thing that dictates how we feel about ourselves and our lives is our state of mind. This deserves maximum prioritization. There is so much deeper, richer life on the other side of the trauma.

Human despair is not mental illness; it's just a normal part of this challenging, precious, priceless human experience. Getting quality therapy and taking it seriously is sacred work, a chance to achieve something from our pain, to come out the other side of the trauma set up to live happier and more successfully for the rest of our lives. That's a worthy goal in and of itself. On top of that, healing ourselves also helps heal our world and that is both a worthy and influential accomplishment.

Part Two

*In the Aftermath of the
Blast Zone—Clearing Away
the Rubble, Moving from
Surviving to Thriving*

CHAPTER 3

Redefine Surrender

"When we are no longer able to change a situation, we are challenged to change ourselves."

—*Viktor E. Frankl*

With those events that shake us to the core, there's much more to it than just making it through the initial blast. The aftershocks and uncertainty can last long after the original event and leave a lot of debris in their wake. In some ways the months just after the immediate crisis can be the most difficult. When the adrenaline and need for immediate action passes, we're left with fewer distractions from the loss and grief and the demons of defeat, hatred, guilt, and despair have more room to run.

In anthropology, in the study of cultures that have clear rites of passage, there is a concept known as the liminal phase which is the point in a profound life-stage ritual in which the initiate has lost his or her old identity and place in society but has not yet been granted the new status and been reintegrated into society. More recently, liminality has crossed over from anthropology into psychology and is used to describe when a person suffers a major life upheaval that shakes him or her loose from their old familiar position in community or society. This is usually a very challenging space for a person to remain in because it is detached from familiar routines and social interactions and support. The sense of liminality, of being in between the old and new way of being, often hits us when we experience sudden, intensely life-changing events. This can happen when a young person moves off to college, when we retire from a career, when someone gets released from prison, or when we suffer a serious prolonged illness, the death of a loved one, a loss of social standing, or bullying and ostracism.

I was a couple of months into my public shaming experience when someone first shared the term liminality with me and I cried as I recognized and resisted the space I'd been forced into. On some subconscious level, I was terrified that the upheaval and uncertainty would be permanent and I'd be trapped in a purgatory of pain and isolation for the rest of my life.

Author and meditation teacher Madisyn Taylor wisely observed that the term "dark night of the soul" is overused and misused. The dark night of the soul isn't just about depression or confusion, but rather it's the place where our lives, and much of what we thought we knew, get turned upside down. It is wildly uncomfortable and can be terrifying. Taylor writes,

We are suddenly shut off from what we thought we had realized and the emotional pain is very real. We may even begin to feel that it was all an illusion and that we are lost forever in this darkness. The more we struggle, the darker things get, until finally we surrender to our not knowing what to do, how to think, where to turn. It is from this place of losing our sense of ourselves as in control that the ego begins to crack or soften and the possibility of light entering becomes real.

My experience was more like one thousand dark nights of the soul, as the legal and financial challenges dragged on and media attacks continued for more than four years. For the first many, many months I was deeply disturbed and often depressed as the train wreck of public shaming careened through my outer life, leaving carnage of my career and reputation.

The hatred toward the reporters who had spread the false allegations and fabricated a narrative about me seared my psyche, and the sense of having been defeated pummeled my already shattered sense of self-worth. When I really paid attention to the overwhelming powerlessness, it terrified me and brought to the surface the unthinkable fear that perhaps I really had been destroyed and just didn't realize it yet.

I reached some terrible depths of despair during those times. *Who the hell was I if I'd never really known myself at all? What if everything I'd ever believed about anything that mattered had been wrong? What if I really wasn't of any value to the world? Was I indeed losing my sanity?*

As someone who had derived much of my own sense of worth through validation from others, there could have been no hotter crucible than an intense, prolonged public shaming. Everywhere I turned I was being told I was no good, of no real value. Every old, buried, and disguised demon of self-doubt reared up, clawing and gnawing my psyche. I felt trapped in the wreckage of my life with no visible escape route. Although I never genuinely contemplated or planned suicide, I did, many times, reach the point where I truly didn't want to wake up. It felt like what I would have to face to make it through the mess was just too hard. But as hard as it was, I could not tolerate the thought of adding additional trauma to John or abandoning my beloved Tessa dog, with whom I had an incredibly tight bond and friendship. I couldn't give up even though I didn't feel like going on.

Thank God and the resiliency muscles I'd already developed, underneath the despair was a tendril of curiosity. The sheer enormity of the mess and devastation of life as I knew it was so shocking and unforeseen, I sensed there had to be some reason, something to be gained from it.

At some subconscious level, I knew this was a time when my survival skills had to shift. Prior to life blowing to pieces, I had relied on a tremendous work ethic, drive, knowledge of the issues I worked on, and good people skills. During my long dark night of the soul, other than people skills, none of those things really helped much. I couldn't force the tangle of circumstances to move any faster no matter how hard I tried. It was impossible to restart my career under the drain of the legal battle and when the media assaults kept skewing Google results away from my professional accomplishments and offerings and onto the allegations and appearance of scandal. Beating my head against the wall, trying to get my work moving in some semblance of what it had looked like before, facing rejection after rejection, left me in despair.

In order to maintain sanity and some hope I needed to learn to disconnect my inner state of being from the circumstances swirling around in my life. My survival was an inside-my-own-head job. A big part of this meant surrendering to the fact that I wasn't going to be able to put my work or myself back together the way it had been before.

Surrender was *not* a natural tendency. I had been raised believing that surrender was weakness, giving up, rolling over, something only for losers. I prided myself on being tough, a fighter, but I was about to learn there is another way, an immeasurably more beautiful way to view surrender.

My first surrender was in accepting that there were aspects of the whole awful mess that truly were beyond my control. I couldn't control what it would do to my career, my reputation, my relationships. I couldn't control the media or openly defend myself against the ugliness being poured forth. I couldn't even control what would happen with my relationship with John. All I could really control was how I handled myself each day, each hour, each moment. My work, goals, and outer journey had been put on pause against my will. I could remain angry and bitter and try to force some sort of action, or I could embrace it as an unexpected sabbatical and lean into the newly opened space to work on my *inner* journey. I chose the latter. That choice may have saved my life; it certainly transformed it, and in the midst of life blowing up, I began blowing open.

The most beautiful surrender came via something of a breakdown. I was at a very low point, overwhelmed and terrified, and had spent a few days nearly comatose, on the couch, ninety-pound Tessa snuggled against me, binge-watching TV, drinking too much beer, fearfully keeping my doors locked and all the shades drawn to stay hidden from the reporters and photographers lurking around my nine-hundred-and-sixty square foot house. Several times they came right up and tried to look in my front window, menacing shadows just a few feet away behind the blind. I stayed very still, like a terrified mouse trying not to catch the eye of the hunting cat.

Finally, one morning, I forced myself to ignore the lure of the couch and remote control, and dragged myself out and slunk down into the tiny hot tub on my deck. It was super cold, single-digit cold. Shell-shocked and totally exhausted, I think my mind finally reached a place where it couldn't race anymore. Something shifted and I became deeply, intensely present in that moment.

Hundreds of times before I had been in that little tub on cold mornings when the steam was billowing thick off the hot water, but I had never *seen* the steam and light before that day. I became aware of rich layers of sound and the silence behind each one. My mind wasn't racing forward, thinking, worrying; it wasn't rummaging backwards, remembering, analyzing. It was just right there, deeply open to the moment. In that instant I lost track of my old, familiar sense of self. I even lost track of the boundary around my physical body. I felt an incredible expansion, a connection, a oneness with a vast and limitless Presence. All fear dropped away and the deepest, purest peace I had ever known washed over me.

In that moment I knew, without doubt, that I was far more than I'd previously believed. I was conscious of my connection to the Source of creation. I would later realize that this was the first time I consciously met my spiritual self and recognized the difference between the little self of ego and the Self of my divine nature, my True Self. Nothing within me would be the same again. I had cracked open.

With all of this swirling, sitting in a weird mix of turmoil, fear, and profound peace, the Christmas holiday season rolled in. John and I were low-key about the holidays, but he had always had a little Christmas tree (often pretty close to a Charlie Brown tree) at his home to provide some special holiday spirit for his son. He had lamented several times that given the chaos, this year, for the first time, he would not have a tree or any decorations.

I decided, albeit very late in the game, that that would not be the case and this set in motion another bit of beauty in the midst of the horror. On December 23, normally a day that I would avoid shopping stores and malls like the Ebola virus, I made my way to Fred Meyer to try to find some sort of small Christmas tree. The remaining cut trees were way too big so I headed to the floral department and there, found one remaining scraggly, foot tall, live potted pine. I bought it and a set of tiny ornaments and then headed to Minto Brown Park for a run with Tessa.

I parked in the lot at the dog park and after Tessa did a bit of dog stuff—sniffing, peeing, and greeting a few other canines—we headed out. The property lies in a flood plain and on this date, given several days of hard rain, many of my usual trails were under water.

After thirty-five minutes, turned back by flooded trails, we were back at the dog park, but I wanted to run for another ten or fifteen minutes so I headed down a service road. Just as we passed the gate into the overgrown dirt road, I heard a hummingbird chattering. I stopped. She was perched on a thin branch over a blackberry bramble several feet in front of me. I took her in for a moment, then took a deep breath and turned to resume my run. When I did, right in front of me, at my feet, on the edge of the road, was a small, perfectly symmetrical cut Christmas tree! How it could have wound up there was an utter mystery and a magical gift.

Back at Mahonia Hall I put the little Charlie Brown potted tree in the kitchen and hid the perfectly shaped "mystery" tree around the corner. When John arrived a little while later, I told him that he would not be having his first Christmas with no tree. I showed him the little live tree and the tiny ornaments I'd purchased and he smiled. "But wait! There's more!" I said and retrieved the mystery tree, explaining what had happened and that he now had a tree for his house for Logan.

That night we decorated the little potted tree in Salem and the following day we decorated the mystery tree at the Portland house. It was the first time in our ten years together we had decorated a tree together. It would *not* be the first year John hadn't had a tree for Logan.

John and I spent Christmas morning together and then I returned to Mahonia Hall, collected the cats, packed some

things, and headed to Bend. I arrived home to a dusting
snow still on the ground. My neighbors had lit the fire fo
me so the little place was already warm when I arrived. I lit
some candles and plugged in the one strand of holiday bubble
lights over the sliding glass door. It was delicious—toasty and
glowing. That night I slept nearly ten hours straight through.

Throughout the holidays the press pounded me and
John and the governor's office and campaign staff. Several of
the *Oregonian's* click-for-cash reporters were relentless. My
attorneys recommended I sue the *Oregonian* to prevent it
from getting my personal emails. That meant suddenly I had
both an investigation by the Oregon Ethics Commission, and
a lawsuit in the Marion County Circuit Court, trying to keep
a dishonest newspaper from getting my personal emails, as
well as a looming federal investigation. The mushroom cloud
just seemed to keep getting bigger and thicker.

In addition to being weary from the constant bombard-
ment and accusations, I was heartsick about what we were
doing to the planet. Virtually all the media across the nation
and beyond was extolling the great news about an uptick in
economic growth and the cheap gas prices. There was no
mention, likely no awareness, that the cheap gas was coming at the cost of tremendous environmental damage from
tar-sand extraction and fracking. There was even less mention, or awareness, of the fact that this type of economic system, which required ever-escalating consumption of natural
resources, was destroying the environment.

My work seemed so small compared to the enormity of
the issues and even that work was now under intense attack by

us media. I hit a deep depression. For two
recliner watching TV and drinking beer,
nally this was a time of the year when
as I'd had for the year just passing and set
e new year ahead. Not this time. I just didn't have
heart for it. This would be the first time I could remember
that I hadn't set goals for the year to come.

I continued to be bombarded by the events swirling through my life—the legal challenges that were a part-time job, trying to get some paid work lined up, and doing what I could to be a support for John. Yet even reeling from all these circumstances, I remained inextricably drawn to the inner work, to the psychological and spiritual shift taking place in my consciousness. I entered a period that proved true the old adage, "When the student is ready, the teacher will appear." One teaching after another turned up in what seemed just the perfect timing for my understanding at that moment. The work and wisdom of Eckert Tolle, Pema Chodron, Michael Singer, Byron Katie, Phillip Moffitt, Christine Greene, Eric Butterworth, and many others. My meditations went much deeper. At some point I started working with *A Course in Miracles* and life changed again.

I had been raised with a heavy-handed, hellfire-and-brimstone form of Christianity. I still vividly remember being a little girl, sitting next to my mom on the crushed red velvet pew in the tiny white church as the pastor blasted out a sermon having something to do with Revelation. With gray, stringy hair flopping, Adam's apple bobbing, and spit flying, the pastor thumped the podium and told us that when we got to heaven there would be streets paved with gold and when the angels sang we would fall on our faces in awe. He said, "One of the rewards of the 'saved' will be watching the 'unsaved' gnash their teeth in hell for eternity."

I looked up at my mom and whispered, "Mom, if that's heaven, I don't want to go." And pretty soon I stopped going to church. In my late teens I rebelled against those teachings and preachings.

Although I continued to explore spirituality, I was vehemently not religious, certainly not Christian, and so I had a lot of resistance when I first cracked open *A Course in Miracles*. Its writings of the Son of God, atonement, communion, the Holy Spirit, and so on unpacked some old baggage, but from the beginning, despite the discomfort, I could sense power in those pages. The *Course* is a body of wisdom that uses Christian terms and concepts for psychotherapeutic purposes. It is both deeply mind-bending and common-sense practical. It describes and explains the split between the ego self and the divine True Self that I was directly experiencing in my life. The *Course* provided language and context for what was happening to me. It was a homecoming.

I hadn't realized it at the time but what I experienced that cold morning in November, and countless times since, was a surrender, the ultimate surrender, to God, Source, Spirit, the Higher Power spoken of in Alcoholics Anonymous. Unlike what I'd believed as a child, this surrender didn't mean giving up my dreams and goals to please an angry God but rather was about awakening to the force, the Divine Mind that supports us at all times and wills our healing and success. What I had believed to be my will was mostly the superficial wants of ego, the little me. At that level we don't even really know what we truly want. My willfulness had in fact kept me playing very small ball.

Our will is only truly free when we reclaim our mind from ego's illusion and littleness, remember who we really are, and begin to see that it's not about sacrificing our own goals to someone else's agenda but realizing we have the willpower of God itself behind our genuine desires. I'd been afraid of sacrificing my free will but in truth had only been sacrificing peace and power.

A Course in Miracles offers:

> *When the light comes and you have said, 'God's Will is mine,' you will see such beauty that you will know it is not of you [in the little you sense of the word]. Out of your joy you will create beauty … The bleak little world will vanish into nothingness, and your heart will be so filled with joy that it will leap into Heaven, and into the Presence of God.*

Bring it on! I would come to see that what I had actually surrendered was my sense of being small, alone, and powerless. I surrendered to the possibility that I was much more than I'd believed even though I didn't know what that meant. Over time I also began learning to surrender unnecessary fear, belief in limits that aren't really there, and ways of being that robbed me of peace and satisfaction. Through surrender I began to find freedom from the bondage of ego.

The field of uncertainty is a difficult place to sit in for very long. If the uncertainty also involves a liminal experience in which our place in society or community has shifted and not yet solidified, the pressure and fear can be overwhelming. Our old world has crumbled, but the new world has not yet emerged. For most of us, in the modern and challenging culture in which we exist, there is tremendous pressure to hurry through the liminal phase, to force into place a new sense of order, even if such order is illusion. Doing so robs us of tremendous opportunity.

Surrendering to the loss of our old identity, the story we told of ourselves and to ourselves, makes room for possibilities that didn't exist, or that we couldn't see, in the old story. This is a point of massive evolutionary potential in how we view our world, others and ourselves, and in how we feel and think. The evolution happens in its own time, sometimes gradually, in small shifts, and sometimes in rapid and profound revelation.

Those times when the mirages of order in our old stories fall to pieces are times when we can *choose* to be diminished, reduced, and limited, or expanded and diversified. The power comes when we resist the fear and urge to contract and instead open to the possibility that the change, no matter how painful, may be the best gift we never imagined. By releasing our death grip on an old, familiar identity we make room for new amazing facets to surface and shine. The most courageous choice is to give time and room to the space between our old story and the new, to sit still in the liminal unknowing and allow the sacred to emerge.

Strategies for Surrendering What
No Longer Serves Us

☞   Do a Can and Can't Control exercise

Some two thousand years ago, a man named Epictetus was born a slave, but due to his brilliance, became a great teacher. He wrote a book that is often referred to as *The Handbook* or *The Art of Living*. Its opening line reads, "*The secret of happiness is knowing that there are some things you can control and some things you cannot.*"

Yep and amen! Wisdom through the ages. The key is to spend our efforts on those things we can control and let the rest go.

On one side of a piece of paper, write down the things you can't control, and on the other side, write the things you can. Now, none of us can really control the future, so just go ahead and put that at the top of the list. That's a biggie, I know. But beyond that, every single time I do this exercise with clients, we identify more actions that are within their control than they realized. For example, here's what this looked like for me during the media attacks.

Can't Control	Can Control
• The future • What the media is going to say • John's reactions to things • What's going to happen in my relationship with John • How the chattering class, political opponents, trolls, or anyone else is going to react to me.	• My inner journey and healing (counseling, exercises) • Healthy habits (exercise, sleep, cut alcohol) • State of being (meditation, presence practice, drawing) • Writing (journal, clean economy bulletins, *Huffington Post* blog) • Whether I grow from this • How I respond to the media misinformation • Build my own social media platform • Explore other options for making a positive contribution (teaching, international work)

This seemingly simple exercise provides a number of benefits. One, it can give some sense of control and having options when we've been feeling utterly powerless. Two, it helps us shift from fixating on the negative and painful aspects of the situation. Three, it can help us see where we've been wasting time and energy on things that are truly beyond our control. This frees us up to identify strategic actions that can actually make a difference in the situation.

☞ Adopt a Meditation Practice

I simply cannot say strongly enough how powerful meditation can be in giving us an opportunity to live more peaceful, empowered, and successful lives. Our minds dictate how we experience life far more than our bodies do.

We have infinitely more power to shift our lens and control our thoughts than we are usually taught to believe. Strategies like becoming aware of the present moment and redirecting when obsessing over the same painful or stressful scene, memory, or fear are useful ways to begin learning to control our thoughts, but the mother lode of benefits comes through regular meditation.

Thank God I'd practiced meditation regularly for years before the crisis hit. I firmly believe it saved my life. Although achieving a meditative state didn't come readily in the early weeks of crisis when my mind was spinning, darting, wildly stressed out, I had enough of a base to make some headway wrestling my thoughts away from the continuous-loop horror show of humiliating memories, breath-catching guilt, and terror.

Meditation adds immeasurably to our ability to be resilient during hardship and even to our ability to make clear decisions that can help us survive. As I was finishing this book, the world was transfixed by the incredible story of survival and rescue of the Thai boys soccer team trapped miles underground in a flooded cave for sixteen days. It is impossible to imagine the tremendous emotional and psychological horror of such an experience. Once details began to emerge, we learned that the young coach of the team, the only adult with the group, had studied as a monk and used his deep expertise in meditation to help the boys stay calm and hopeful in truly nightmarish conditions. If it worked for them in that terrifying situation, surely it could have some benefit for what you are facing right now.

Through deepening my meditation practice I got to the point where when someone would ask me how I was doing, I could say honestly, if a little cheekily, "You know, it's amazing what a peaceful, pleasant day one can have while sitting in the midst of an open FBI investigation!"

There is a reason why virtually every major wisdom tradition includes some version of meditation. More recently science is getting on board as research shows that even short periods of meditation change brain waves, increasing relaxation and reducing anxiety and depression. Studies have shown that people who have meditated regularly for several months produce less of the stress hormone cortisol. In fact, there is now a large body of evidence showing that meditation has profound effects on our bodies, having been proven to reverse heart disease, reduce pain, and boost the immune system.

An even deeper aspect of meditation is that it provides a portal to the aspects of ourselves we often fail to recognize. Through meditation it becomes easier to notice that we aren't our thoughts; instead, we are the ones who are observing those thoughts and are able to change them. Meditation can help us remember that aspect of us that is much more than the bodies we wear. It is as though, in the silence, we enter into collaboration with God or Source. It provides a chance to experience a sense of self much bigger and more powerful than the ego self we have attached to. In the long months of my ordeal my meditation practice deepened enormously and I regularly tapped into the awesome sense of expansion and connection that I first experienced that cold morning in my little hot tub. Meditation helped me remember that I wasn't alone after all.

Starting a regular meditation practice doesn't have to be complicated or terribly time-consuming. It doesn't mean you have to quit your job and join a monastery or become a monk! You can, in fact, start very simply. Even a few minutes a day can have measurable benefits. In the time it takes you to put your clothes on in the morning, you can begin to clothe your mind in peace, release, and relief.

I understand that it is particularly hard to start learning to meditate when sitting in the middle of traumatic events, but there is nothing to lose and only peace and strength to gain. If reinvention is a significant part of your challenge, whether of career, relationships, or your own personal identity, meditation is a powerful tool to help clear away the clutter, find clarity, and truly figure out what it is you want from the next phase of your life.

Sometimes, when life drives us to our knees, the best option is to stay there a while, listen, check in with our heart, give in, and go in to that deep inner space we might not have visited before. True surrender is not about giving up; it's about opening up, allowing for new awareness and possibility, perhaps granting access to power and levels of support we hadn't known existed. Then when we get back to our feet we can take some of this new depth with us into every facet of our life and work.

We are, in essence, like trees; our growth takes place in the softer inner core and then pushes outward. Deeply shattering experiences can break open old, thick, protective bark, allowing for new movement and expansion. An egg cracked from the outside dies, but cracked open from the inside reveals a new life. Life is lived from the inside out. Sometimes it takes life pounding us down for us to slow enough to retreat inward and surrender to the immeasurable beauty of our own souls. The moment of surrender is not the end; it's when life really begins. True surrender is an act of strength and awesome power that allows us to be born anew.

CHAPTER 4

Sticky People and Fallen Leaves

"Losing so many others hurt more than I would have believed but it also gave me the chance to really find my Self."

—Cylvia Hayes

When the first few said, "Well, you're going to find out who your friends really are," I didn't pay it much mind. In the early days of the media barrage, I mostly locked myself away, Tessa always by my side, in the official governor's residence—known as Mahonia Hall—too embarrassed, terrified and freaked out to go out into public. Somewhat comforted by the fact that the official residence was guarded and secure, I tried to numb the pain by binge-watching television, carefully avoiding the news channels with the relentless hyped-up narrative and speculation about me, the governor, and the crisis blowing through our lives. During those terrible days I checked my emails and social media accounts dozens of times a day because so many people were sending me kind, supportive messages and notes. A few sent flowers or thoughtful gifts. Because I was so desperate for validation and violently frustrated by the inability to defend myself, those little gifts and kind words meant the world to me.

However, as days dragged into weeks and it became clear the story, the spectacle, wasn't going away, more and more of the supporters did. Either they just got back to their own busy lives or they became fearful they'd somehow wind up with targets on their own backs if they stayed close to me. The abandonment was stunningly painful. I am someone who needs more alone time than anyone I know and so was completely unprepared for the shock and pain of being rejected by most of the people I had considered friends or colleagues.

Still not understanding the full seriousness of the events that had been set in motion, I wanted to reach out to some of my closer colleagues and clients. I wanted to apologize for the mess I had caused by not being transparent about my past, but my attorneys told me not to do it. They said the federal agents were likely to interview many of those people and if they wanted to they could make the case that I was apologizing for the allegations of corruption or even trying to influence witnesses. I couldn't believe it and found myself wondering fearfully, *What would be the outcome if the investigators reacted in the same sensational and accusatory manner as the media was doing?* In addition, I was no longer welcome at the state capital as the governor's staff scrambled to cope with the media assaults and public records requests.

Not long after, on a day when John and I were together at home, I got a phone call from a colleague I had trusted. He asked me to resign from my position on the Board of Directors of the American Leadership Forum Oregon. He was worried the media would come after the organization because of my involvement. I asked if they'd been contacted by the press and he said, "No, but I just don't want to go there." I loved the Leadership Forum and had poured myself into it. I had made several what I believed to be very close friends through my work with the organization. Not one of my fellow board members stood up for me or thanked me for my years of service. This abandonment and willingness to throw me away cut to the quick and at that moment it felt as though the media assault was taking everything from me—my reputation, my work, my relationships, my identity.

When I got off the phone, I crumbled into deep, spine-wracking sobs. John held me. As my tears and shudders began to ease, he reached out and stroked my forehead and said, "You're a beautiful person, Cylvia. You care so deeply about things." Part of me was deeply grateful for his support; part of me felt wholly unworthy of it.

One of my great terrors at that time had been that my mess would cost John the election but, to my tremendous relief, he won reelection despite all the false allegations. And yet the media feeding frenzy showed no signs of slowing down. Still trying to do his job and govern through the mess left him exhausted and constantly, massively stressed. He had little left for me and, in truth, I was so consumed by guilt that I was uncomfortable being around him.

Overnight I had lost my entire professional network, which made up the vast majority of people I interacted with. I lost the professional work I'd been engaged in and the projects I'd been leading as First Lady. I'd lost my place in society. I retreated to my little home and spent hours and days on end alone three hours from the capital and John. My picture continued to be plastered all over the media and I didn't feel safe going out in public. I had never felt so alone. I just hadn't realized how much I needed people until so many disappeared.

Abandonment and gradual withdrawal of old acquaintances is a common experience for people in the process of recovering and reinventing after a heavy life blow. It is a pile-on of pain to be sure, the loss of trust and support compounding the trauma. For me, already burning with shame and humiliation, deeply questioning my value, the brutal truth that most people actually didn't value me enough to stick around cut to the bone, and the humiliation deepened as more people fled. I began to wonder if I truly had any genuine friends, anyone who cared about me beyond the influential position I'd been in. Over time, I would learn that it wasn't that I didn't have true friends; I'd just been largely unaware of who they were.

You can't lose a true friend; those that leave us in our hour of genuine need weren't genuine friends to begin with. I decided to just cut loose those who chose not to stick—even if we shared DNA. There is no point in attempting to win back the affection of someone who doesn't have enough love for us or strength of character to stand with us through hardship, to be there when we need them most. It is a powerful decision to let them go, but as I explain in the next chapter, there is great power in doing so without hatred because forgiveness is a potent survival strategy.

There's a reason we come together for a time. There is even a reason for the hurt we feel when we are left behind or when we leave. When a tree sheds its old leaves, they fall to the ground and become nutrients, enriching the soil and the next round of growth. The same can be true of all the old leaves of our pasts. They fertilize the soil of our souls, prepping the grounds for rich, vital new sprouts, giving us nourishment to grow forward. We release ourselves when we release them.

On the flip side of the coin, we may be surprised by those who do step forward when we are at our lowest points. They may be family, old friends, acquaintances, or even just kind strangers. These are the people strong enough to sit with our pain, to stick even when we might not be so great to be around. Often they are people of special depth and compassion because they've experienced their own deep traumas. These "sticky people" are priceless.

Very early in the ordeal, on a Saturday, I saw a familiar Oklahoma prison phone number come up on my phone several times in rapid succession. Jonathan was the son of my late older sister who died from addiction to opioids. I had had custody of him for a time in his teens but couldn't handle him and sent him back to Oklahoma DHS, one of the most painful decisions of my life. Still, I stayed in regular contact with him and supported him as he dealt with serving a prison sentence, getting clean, and getting his GED.

For some mystical reason, he and I loved each other from the first time we met when he was an infant. That love had never faded. He was, in fact, the closest thing I had to a child.

In order to have phone calls with him in prison, I kept money in a collect-call account. He could only call at certain times, and he usually did so every Saturday. Given my demanding schedule, I often couldn't take his call on the first try. I had learned from experience that when he tried repeatedly over a short amount of time, it usually meant there was a problem on his end.

That day I hadn't wanted to talk with him for two reasons. First, I had to tell him what was going on with me. I felt it would be hypocritical not to. He was someone I was trying to help and mentor through his jail time, but my life had just blown up due to choices I myself had made that could have landed me in jail. Second, I knew he was a worrier with strong family loyalty and I knew he would be very worried about me and not even be able to stay in communication about it very well. After all, the collect calls were limited to fifteen minutes.

On the next ring, feeling too guilty to ignore it, I answered. After several minutes catching me up on what had been happening in his life, he paused to ask how I was doing and I told him the story. He was surprisingly calm and supportive. He already knew a lot about my past and what I had had gone through and in many ways he'd been through far worse. He said, in his colorful jail-ese language, that everybody made mistakes and the haters that were hatin' on me had all made mistakes of their own. They were only coming after me because I was doing something with my life and they wanted to tear it down. He said one thing he knew was that I was a good person. He had never seen me intentionally hurt anybody, only try to help, and in fact I was the only one who had always been there for him.

He was sticking with me for sure, and I was surprised how much his support and love meant to me. He called again the next day. It was unusual for him to call two days in a row, and again, I didn't want to take his call, but I knew he was worrying, so I answered. He was wonderfully supportive, even protective.

Toward the end of the fifteen minutes I told him that I hadn't wanted to take the call because I didn't want to talk to *anybody* just then, but I took it because I knew he'd be stressed and wanted to reassure him. But the truth was the call had reassured and comforted me. I thanked him with deep sincerity and I could feel him shift a little bit. He said, "Yeah, Aunt Cylvia. I love you. Anything I can do to help."

Looking back, I realize it was the first time in our relationship that I had genuinely thanked him, that I had been the receiver and he had been the one to give. This was one of the first of many bright spots that would pop through the darkness of those first days as the exchange would prove to be a powerful progression in a relationship that would become increasingly important and central in the months to come.

When the magnitude of my media shaming really dawned on me, I feared it would be impossible to overcome. I wondered if I would have to leave the Pacific Northwest or even the country in order to be able to work or reclaim myself as something other than what the media had constructed.

During that dark time in my life, Monica Lewinsky made the brave move of stepping into public again. She delivered a courageous TED talk about her experience as ground zero for online bullying. The talk and her courage touched my heart. I realized that in her case there was virtually nowhere, in the United States at least, that she could have gone without changing her name, where her public shaming wouldn't follow. I was so impressed she'd made it through that horror as a twenty-two-year-old woman being chewed up and spit out by some of the most powerful political forces in the country and was still committed to doing something with her life. I wanted to meet her.

In an amazing series of events, one of my "sticky" colleagues knew Monica and put us in touch. Monica was gracious enough to accept my request for a call. While our conversation is our own, I will say I was impressed with her before that call; I was much more so after.

As human beings we are genetically hardwired for connection with fellow human beings. When we lived in roaming tribes, being exiled was usually a death sentence because it was almost impossible to physically survive alone against the predators and elements. That cellular memory is still alive within us, which is why being shunned, ridiculed, and exiled evokes such a deeply primal terror. Shame researcher Brené Brown has said, "A sense of belonging is the biggest driver of human behavior." This is a large part of why it is hard to sit in the unmoored liminal stage of massive life change.

Being humiliated or shamed in front of others, especially entire social groups such as classmates, colleagues, one's hometown, or the public at large is a terrifying, devastating experience. Neuroscience reveals that the psychological wound of being exiled stimulates the same part of the brain that is activated when we suffer a physical wound. The trauma is real and triggers the same stress chemicals as being physically threatened. These experiences create tremendous anxiety and feelings of being isolated, alone, panicked, and hopeless. It's easy to believe that our lives, relationships, and place in society have been irrevocably damaged and there is no real way forward. This is dangerous territory and needs to be taken seriously.

Without intentional treatment and professional and familial support, the outcomes can be destructive, even deadly. This is why suicide, especially in young people, is all too often associated with shaming and bullying experiences. Nelson Mandela was noted to have said, "I learned that to humiliate another person is to make him suffer an unnecessarily cruel fate." If you or a loved one are being bullied or rejected during a time of need, take the wound seriously and get professional help if necessary.

As I mentioned earlier, getting professional therapy was one of the things that may have saved me in the early weeks of my exile. Another thing was reaching out for connection. Something in me knew I was at a dangerous level of isolation and needed community, and because I was in a process of profound reflection and spiritual deepening, it seemed natural to return to the Unity spiritual community I had been part of many years earlier.

Feeling like the prodigal daughter, I nervously stepped into the little sanctuary I hadn't visited in over a decade. There were certainly some turning heads and curious stares, but mostly there was support, compassion, and genuine concern. I felt welcome, but also very vulnerable, and fought back tears through the entire service.

After attending Unity services a number of times, the minister asked to meet with me. She asked if I would tell a bit of my story and share some of the insights that had been surfacing at an upcoming Sunday service. She said she thought it would be good for the congregation. I thought, "*Oh geez. She wants to address the elephant in the room and that elephant is me. Ughh.*" I didn't want to do it, but I respected her wisdom, certainly didn't want to be a distraction to the group, and I believed she wouldn't ask me if she didn't think it was safe.

That Sunday morning I was surprisingly calm as I walked up to the stage. My only nervousness was whether or not I'd be able to hold back the tears—at that point I still wasn't comfortable crying in public. I began to speak about the traumatic events I had been experiencing and some of the deep insights that were beginning to shine through and, as feared, the tears came. Beautifully, so did a box of tissues lovingly supplied by one of the congregants. Many, some with tears in their own eyes, nodded encouragement. At the end they stood in applause, not for the quality of the talk but to show their support. It was a step toward healing and I suspect the minister had known it would be all along.

Amazingly, a few years later, I am not only a leader and regular Sunday speaker in that community but am enrolled in Unity Worldwide Ministerial School! I never would have seen that one coming. Over time, reconnecting with that community and spiritual path would turn out to be massive collateral beauty, rising out of the shrapnel of my old life and identity.

Another beautiful gem was the transformation of my relationship with my mother. I was ten days into my public shaming before I called her, nervous as I dialed; it was not my practice to turn to her when I needed comfort and I had no idea how she was going to react to the mess I was sitting in. She floored me with her fierce protectiveness and kindness. She said reporters had contacted her several times but she had either not returned their calls or told them "no comment!" She told me, with greater fervor than ever before in my adult life, that she was proud of me and respected what I had done with my life. She ranted about how "mean and nasty" the media was and that she wouldn't have anything to do with them.

Her words of love and support flowed over me like drops of warm rain, or salt tears. I found myself wanting to share with her how the attacks were triggering, once again, in a devastatingly powerful and inescapable way, the deep, dark family traumas that I had worked so hard to heal from. This had always been something of a landmine subject in my family but that day, lonely and wounded, my need overwhelmed me and I opened up to her.

She just listened, intently, warmly. And then she blew my mind when she said, "You know those experiences from our childhood really affect us. I'm seventy-seven years old and I am dealing with that from my own childhood right now." She had just lost her husband of nineteen years two months earlier and was struggling to overcome the fear of living alone due to events and programming she'd received as a young girl.

I was astounded and grateful she would share that with me. It was one of the deepest, most mutually supportive communications we had ever had. At that moment I just needed my mama and she was there.

Just a few days later, she betrayed me. Or so I thought.

The *Oregonian* ran yet another story attacking me and in it my mother had been speaking to a reporter. I was devastated. Although her public comments were supportive and defensive of me, I just couldn't believe she would speak to the media after promising not to and without at least telling me.

I stewed over it, unable to focus on much of anything else, feeling brutally betrayed. Finally I called to beg her not to talk to any more reporters.

When she answered the phone, she sounded nervous and quickly explained that the guy had just shown up at her front door and it upset and scared her. She tried telling him she had just lost her husband and was very uncomfortable with him being there but he just kept at her, explaining that he was there on behalf of the *Oregonian.*

My blood boiled. Because she hadn't responded to their inquiries, the *Oregonian* had sent a man out to ambush her on her doorstep. My mother was a seventy-seven-year-old woman who had just lost her husband, was in mourning, fearful living alone, and those vultures had sent a strange man to her door! I seethed at the heartless lack of compassion all in an effort to stir up additional clickbait.

Nervously, Mom said, "Cylvia, I am very, very sorry. I didn't know how to get him to stop. It's just not in my nature to shut the door in someone's face." Instantly, my anger melted into compassion and guilt.

"Oh, Mom," I said, "I'm so sorry my mess has hurt you like this." From down beneath old, tired wounds and layers of armor, a forgotten fierce urge to protect her surged to the surface. It has been with me ever since. I hadn't realized the treasure I'd been keeping buried.

Months later, as the dust settled a bit and the trial-by-media and public shaming moved out of the acute phase into chronic, drawn-out legal processes, I decided to take a big road trip back to Oklahoma to visit my mom, and my nephew who had not had a visitor in the four years he had been in prison.

My plan was to car camp along the way to Oklahoma and probably even set up my tent on my mom's lovely front yard while I was there. The trick was packing a 2005 Prius for a two-week car camping trip with a large, extremely pampered hound dog occupying the entire back seat.

My approach to packing the car was to arrange things in "rooms." The back seat, of course, was Tessa's couch. The passenger seat and floorboard was my office and library, holding my laptop, journal, sketch pad, and numerous books on spiritual growth, new economics, and trial-by-media. Some of these included *Nature's Wealth*, *An Unfettered Soul*, *Authentic Spirituality*, and *So You've Been Publicly Shamed*. On top of this, within easy access, was a stack of maps of the US and several of the states we'd be traveling through.

Behind the front seats I had packed the floorboard with two cases of good Oregon IPA beer, a bag of Tessa's kibble, hiking boots, and backpack. On top of that, behind the passenger seat, I wedged my "kitchen." This was a plain but extra sturdy cardboard box that held my single-burner stove, three small propane canisters, two small stacking pots and one Teflon fry pan, a small wood cutting board with a handle, a blue plastic bowl and blue plastic plate, an assortment of mismatched silverware, a scrub brush and dish soap. It also held a hatchet, some newspaper for starting a fire, and my small LED lantern. Over all this I placed my folding recliner camp chair because I wanted to be able to get to it easily. The final cherry topper was a small bowl of Tessa's kibble in case she got hungry during our long drives.

The hatchback contained my "sink"—six gallon jugs of water pressed right up against the back of the back seat in a little gap left by my "fridge" and "pantry"—the ice chest and a small, square cardboard box filled with dry food such as cereal, wheat crackers, sardines, jars of tuna fish, canned chili, etc. On this rested my "closet" consisting of my gym bag filled with running and hiking clothes, running shoes and my knee brace, and a leather duffel bag filled with my regular and camp clothes and toiletries. All around these things, in every nook and cranny in the hatchback, I stuffed the "bedroom"— the tent, my sleeping bag, Tessa's sleeping bag, the fleece bag liner that I loved to snuggle in in the mornings and evenings in camp, and two fairly flat pillows (these were both for me— not Tessa, though I often found her in the tent lying on them). All of these items, save for Tessa's bag, I put into sturdy black garbage bags to try to keep them as clean as possible.

The most challenging part of the bedroom was the two Thermarest sleeping pads (one for me and one for Tess). In order to be able to make camp quickly I did not want to travel with these deflated and stuffed into their carrier bags. So I inflated each about three quarters full and squished them carefully alongside the entire passenger side of the car, wedging them between the front passenger seat and the front and back passenger doors, with one end tucked under the dashboard and the other wedged against the ceiling by the hatchback. This would obscure Tessa's view from that side, but she usually stuck her head out the driver side back window so I figured she'd tolerate it.

The "bathroom" was the final necessity. The toilet consisted of a small orange plastic trowel and a couple of rolls of toilet paper. And finally, the "shower." This was a plastic sun shower that I had had for nearly twenty years. It was a tough, thick plastic sack of water, clear on one side with a black background beneath that, with a handle for hanging on the top and a tube with a plastic faucet on the bottom. Once filled with water and laid in the sun with the clear side up, the dark background beneath the water collected solar heat.

The epic journey is a story unto itself. We camped in unmarked, beautiful places, usually without another human soul in sight. I drove long distances, most often without even having the radio on, just thinking, listening inwardly, being. Tessa slept or held her head out the window, taking in all the new scents.

On the seventh day as I neared my mom's place I felt increasingly uneasy, always unsure how things would go with a family encounter. Mom was waiting for me at the end of the long driveway. I got out and gave her a long, warm hug. It felt different than in times past.

The house smelled strongly of cleaning products and it looked enormously better than the last time I'd been there. Mom said she'd been cleaning for the past few days, getting all ready for our visit. She had also gone to the beauty shop and had her hair done. I realized that she, too, had been nervous about the visit and my heart went out to her.

Tessa didn't care whether it was clean or not; she was just delighted to be out of the car, off the ground, and on a big soft couch again.

My younger brother and his fiancée showed up the following day. Over the next two days our family enjoyed the most pleasant time together I had known in my adult life. Mom would later say that with that big hug I'd given her in the driveway it felt like I had accepted her back as my mama. I didn't realize it at the time but that is exactly what I had done.

On day nine of the trip I situated a very displeased Tessa with a family friend and her amorous poodle, Willy, and made my way to Lawton, a for-profit prison with a terrible reputation, to visit my nephew.

It took about half an hour to get checked in, as there were about half a dozen people in the waiting room ahead of me. Others came in after me. Most were African American or Hispanic and mostly women accompanying little kids waiting to see their daddies. It was very sad.

Finally, I was taken through the metal detectors, pat-downs, razor-wire walkways, and multiple gates.

Jonathan was seated at one of the square tables, eyes straight forward and down. As I approached from his side, he saw me and stood up. We hugged hard. As soon as I sat down across from him, my eyes filled with tears. He said, "Don't cry. You gotta be strong." But I couldn't keep it in check. As I struggled to get my emotions settled, his face softened and he said, "It's okay, take a minute."

My eyes met the eyes of a young black woman at the next table. She nodded knowingly. I said, "It's been a very long time since we've seen one another." She nodded again.

Finally, my tears abated. I was so relieved that he looked good, still young and handsome. He still had a twinkle to his eyes.

We talked a little bit and then he said with great earnestness, "It is so good to see you. I can't believe you came all this way to see me."

I said, "I love you, Jonathan. I always have."

"I love you too, Aunt Cylvia. I just can't believe you came all this way. Thank you so much."

Jonathan and I talked about all sorts of things; his history, his thoughts about what he wanted to do when he got out of prison, my trial-by-media situation. I learned a number of new things about him and he would probably say the same of me. I told him of the ordeal it took to get through security to see him and how I was such a newbie and didn't know which blue door to go through.

He said he'd had a similar experience being unsure where he was supposed to go to get to the visitation room. It was a first for him as well. It struck me as so sad that he had been in prison for four years and this was the first visit he'd had.

A typical visit is two hours but because I had come in from so far away, we had been given a four-hour window. I couldn't imagine that we would want to sit there at a small table for four hours but we wound up using every last minute until the guard came and told us time was up. Another long hug and Jonathan was escorted back to his cell block as I made my way through the series of steel doors and gates and concrete and wire. I was so glad I'd made the effort to visit with him.

By the way Tessa greeted me when I arrived to pick her up one would have thought she'd been the one in prison for years! She yowled and whined and wrapped her long body around my legs, and leaped up on me far more than she ever had before. She had dealt with snakes, mosquitos, ticks, and catfish, but nothing was as relentless as Willy the humpety-hump horndog poodle.

She was more than happy to get back into the Prius. We headed due west back toward Oregon and my beloved little home. We still had a lot of miles to cover. We camped, hiked, swam in rivers, experienced magnificent landscapes. My thoughts moved back and forth between the horrific events still embroiling my life and work and the beautiful experience I'd just had with my family. I felt very peaceful and full-hearted.

After four thousand five-hundred and sixty-nine miles, fourteen days, and nine states, I arrived safely and joyfully at my little Bend home—no injuries; no mechanical problems. In hindsight this was only one of many homecomings throughout the trip. I had opened my heart and allowed the homey feeling of "Mama" to seep back in. I now knew I had a safe space there. I had given Jonathan the gift of contact with me, the only person who had really been a mama in his life. The shaming had put me into a paring-down process. Being stripped of identity, facing ego, and returning home to my essential, authentic self and that trip, immersed in nature and family history, moved the process forward. I had made strides toward the deep inner home of my spirit, the I Am.

When I stopped the car and opened the door, Tessa went immediately into the kitchen and flopped full length onto her side on the cool kitchen floor. As I came up to her, she didn't even lift her head but cracked her comical canine grin and thumped her tail against the linoleum. She was happy to be back in the dog house, our house.

My mother stuck with me through the entire stretch of life blowing to pieces, with unflagging love, encouragement, and fierce protectiveness. She visited me in Oregon for the first time. She has become my friend, confidant, and spiritual advisor and, amazingly, sometimes even asks me for advice. She is eighty-one as I write this and I am immeasurably grateful we found our way back to one another even if it took catastrophe to bring it about.

My nephew and I still had a lot of ground to cover in the months to come, which I describe in later chapters, and in many ways we stuck with each other like no other, building one of the most important relationships for each of us.

The relationships in our lives cycle in, through and out. Very few last the duration and that's okay. The people in our lives, and the roles they fill reflect our level of consciousness at that time. Sometimes this brings new ways of relating, and sometimes it means moving on and choosing not to relate at all. Modern Chinese mystic Zhao noted that, "In most of our human relationships we spend much of our time reassuring one another that our costumes of identity are on straight." As we evolve, our identities evolve and our relationships will often shift. The mighty maple tree is at its most splendid in autumn as its old, dying parts are falling away like golden rain.

Sometimes shedding an untrustworthy person is permanent and sometimes it's not. My mom and I went years with little communication; I needed space to heal some things from our past and make some changes and she did as well. After that separation we found our way back to one another from a place of love and mutual respect. Sometimes, a relationship needs to be set aside for a while to be picked up later once one or both people have moved to a new level of being.

Often, in the quiet but disquieting aftermath of lost relationships, we get a chance to go deeper with the most important relationship of all—the one we have with our Selves.

Strategies for Building True Friends and Genuine Community

☞   Cut loose those who leave; cultivate those who stick

Going through a prolonged, intense, seismic life event is like running a marathon. Some people will show up at the starting line. A few will join for stretches in the middle. Very, very few will run the whole course by your side. Those beautiful few who don't shy away from the starting gun, who are there to pick you up when you stumble midway through, and who celebrate you at the finish line are precious and priceless. Cherish them and let them know how much they mean to you. And stay open to new supporters, from unusual sources. The Universe is sending you love and support all the time. Be sure to keep an eye out for it.

Here is an exercise to help with this. Make a list of your sticky people. Those who have or currently are offering genuine support while you are going through a major challenge. Who has given you a ride to the hospital, or brought you a meal? Who picks up the phone proactively to check in on you? Who do you turn to in order to share a deep hurt? Who has been there in genuine celebration when you have accomplished something? Who are people in the past who are no longer living that offered you unconditional love or support when you needed it? Write down their names. Next, take some time to feel gratitude for each of these important people. Finally, write a note, send an email, offer a prayer, even make a phone call thanking them for their invaluable contribution to your life. Acknowledge them and practice gratitude.

☞   Proactively build community

If the isolation is really deep or public (like in a shaming or bullying), be sure to proactively reach out even if it's to groups that are new to you. Connecting or reconnecting with a spiritual home can be extraordinarily helpful during times of trauma. Volunteering is another great way to start rebuilding community and I'll share a bit more on that in a later chapter.

☞   Become a better friend

One of the things my ordeal helped me see was that I really hadn't been a very good friend. I was reliable. I'd have people come to me with their confidences and when the chips were really down for someone, I would step up. However, I wasn't a proactive friend. I didn't invest much in my friendships. That has changed because I have learned how precious true friendship really is and I no longer take these beautiful treasures for granted. As I am becoming a better friend, I am earning better friends and stronger friendships in return.

I was deeply hurt by a few people I really expected to stick who didn't, and deeply touched by some of the unexpected ones who did. Aside from John, my circle of friends and close confidants is almost unrecognizable from before the public shaming. My sticky people loved me through some of the hardest experiences of my life. They were a refuge. They fed my body, carrying homemade meals to my front door without saying a word because they knew I was grieving and wanted to be alone. They fed my spirit, listening, gently counseling, and affirming my value in moments when I questioned whether I had any. They occasionally kicked my butt when I was wallowing too long or unable to see what I had to be grateful for. They will probably never fully understand how much their unflagging support meant and still means to me. I am so, so grateful.

When we are moving through bullying, shame, extreme isolation, or any major life challenge and change, the point is to *move* forward and to reach out. Those are not times to just go it alone. For most of us it isn't easy to ask for help, to allow our wounds to show. There's such terror that if we reveal our vulnerability and self-perceived imperfections, others will retract their approval. This is usually another of those fears based solely on imagined outcomes and false beliefs. Moving past that fear, opening up to others, is how we form genuine relationships and touch lives including our own.

In the aftermath of major life changes, we may never regain the friends we thought we had. We may never be invited back into the groups, circles, and communities we once belonged to, and that hurts. But there is a whole, big, wide world out there that doesn't know or care about anything we've done in the past or anything anyone has said about us. There are pathways, opportunities, and new friends beyond the ordeal—even, perhaps, because of the ordeal—beyond imagining.

CHAPTER 5

Forgive

"Forgiving is rediscovering the shining path of peace that at first you thought others took away when they betrayed you."

—*Dodinsky*

Life has presented me with lots of opportunities to practice forgiveness, probably because I was so darned bad at it. At the same time I was gaining greater appreciation for the people who were stepping up for me, I was seething with hatred for those who had orchestrated the public shaming and smear campaign. I was shocked at the depth of animosity I carried and how intensely I wanted them to hurt like they had hurt me. My hatred and the white-hot fury that they were getting away with, even being rewarded for their mistreatment of me, consumed my thoughts, kept me awake at night, and stole God knows how many moments of peace.

The person I held the most hatred toward was the *Willamette Week* reporter who had kicked the whole public shaming and false allegations into motion. This was in no small part because the man had been trying to destroy me for years. In August 2010, during John's campaign to return as Oregon's governor, this reporter began publishing allegations that I had been given a small subcontract with the Oregon Department of Energy because I was then-girlfriend of the likely next governor. That was the first time I found myself in the midst of an ugly, accusatory, sensationalized media frenzy. The allegations were bogus but they led to investigations of several Department of Energy employees and me. All were eventually exonerated and the head of the department wound up winning an unprecedented million-dollar settlement against the State of Oregon for violating his civil rights by putting him under criminal investigation.

Despite being cleared of the reporter's false allegations, the Department of Energy investigation lasted well into my first year as First Lady, casting a shadow over everything I tried to do. And here he was again, with me at the center of his bull's-eye of ego-driven BS.

Early on I would actually fantasize about running him and some of the dishonest *Oregonian* reporters down with a car or having someone discover that they had molested children so that they would go through their own horrific public shaming. Sick, I know. Even as I was doing it, I knew it was sick. Thank goodness my Higher Self always stepped in and I would remember that I didn't really want to put more of that kind of ugliness into our world. I was pretty sure that if I saw one of these guys trapped in a burning building, I'd try to get him out. Pretty sure.

I was caught in a state of intense discord. On the one hand I was experiencing deep spiritual insights, teachings, and awakenings and I could sense a layer of beauty and truth beneath everyday appearances. But on the other hand I was experiencing an intensity of hatred that was overpowering and consuming. I wanted to stop hating but didn't know how.

The first breakthrough came while reading the *Book of Forgiving*, written by Desmond Tutu and his daughter Mpho. This beautiful book shares their experience and wisdom in navigating personal forgiveness for unthinkable acts and the incredible national process of forgiveness South Africa undertook in the wake of the atrocities of apartheid. In the introduction, they offer a *Prayer Before the Prayer*:

I want to be willing to forgive
But I dare not ask for the will to forgive
In case you give it to me
And I am not ready
I am not ready for my heart to soften
I am not ready to be vulnerable again
Not yet ready to see that there is humanity
in my tormentor's eyes
Or that the one who hurt me may also have cried
I am not yet ready for the journey
I am not interested in the path
I am at the prayer before the prayer of forgiveness

Grant me the will to want to forgive
Grant it to me not yet but soon
Can I even form the words
Forgive me?
Dare I even look?
Do I dare see the hurt I have caused?
I can glimpse the shattered pieces of that fragile thing
That soul trying to rise on the broken wings of hope
But only out of the corner of my eye
I am afraid of it
And if I am afraid to see
How can I not be afraid to say
Forgive me?
Is there a place where we can meet?
You and me
The place in the middle
The no man's land
Where we straddle the lines
Where you are right
And I am right too
And both of us are wrong and wronged
Can we meet there?
And look for the place where the path begins
The path that ends when we forgive.

Something in me knew that forgiveness was essential to healing and I believed I'd been working on it for months before I encountered the *Prayer Before the Prayer*. That's when I realized I'd been mistaken. As I read that prayer, I knew that I wasn't truly willing to forgive them. Forgiving my attackers seemed completely unjustified, undeserved, and phony; it was letting them off the hook. And that was scary. If I let them off the hook, was I then on it? I had a lot invested in blaming them, in seeing them and having others see them as the bad guys. Somebody other than me just had to be responsible for the terrible mess in my life, for the pain I was suffering.

What this meant, of course, was that I was attached to being a victim. *Yuck.* The moment I let this in, I knew the truth of the line I'd heard somewhere that said hating someone, or clinging to resentment, is like drinking rat poison and expecting the other guy to die. I knew I was poisoning myself. I knew my burning desire for justice and vengeance was only searing my wounds open again and again, preventing healing, but I didn't know how to stop.

I had to start (a little unconvincingly, even to myself) with affirming, "*Okay, I'm willing to become willing even though I don't really like it.*" I didn't really yet believe those turkeys deserved my forgiveness but I knew *I* needed it. Each time I'd feel the hatred flare up, each time one of my attackers posted another spun and ugly story or I had to spend all day dealing with the legal implications of the false allegations, I would say to myself, "*Hatred is not who you are. You are more powerful than that.*" I can't begin to recall how many thousands of times I uttered this. It was weak, but it was all I had just then.

Each time the hatred flared, I said to myself, "*Choose again. I am willing to forgive.*" Over time, almost without my noticing, the knot of hatred began to fray around the edges a little. As it did, I was able to work with stronger forgiveness techniques like loving-kindness meditation, the exercises at the end of this chapter, and holding my attackers in positive prayer. As it turns out, praying for our so-called enemies is also praying for our own freedom.

I also began to have opportunities to face those I hadn't forgiven.

One incident drove home the awesome power and potential in genuine forgiveness, of choosing to loosen my hold on the need for making someone else wrong. When I lost my position of perceived influence, scores of people abandoned me. A few of those who fled I had considered dear friends and was deeply hurt by their abandonment. I felt used, lied to, and embarrassingly naïve. Forgiveness was not flowing.

Over a year into the public shaming, one of these people left a message asking to get together. My wounded self responded with the following email:

> *Greetings _____ ,*
>
> *I received your message and decided it was time to let you know that I was deeply hurt by your disappearance during my ordeal. It very much feels to me that you were interested in me when I had access and influence and when those things were gone, so were you. I have grown so, so much this past year and a half and one of the things I have learned is to be much more intentional about the people I spend time with. I have realized that I was surrounded by a lot of disingenuous, inauthentic people. I have shed those and have nurtured those who are real as people and genuine as friends.*

I still love you, but I no longer trust our relationship.

I hope you find peace,
Cylvia

Okay, that's a little embarrassing. It's nicely worded and all, but good grief, it's such an obvious effort to hit back. I was accusing her of being a lousy, cowardly friend and was taking the opportunity to reject her in return. This was using forgiveness as a weapon! Clearly, the big growth I'd mentioned hadn't included much in the way of forgiving old friends.

To her credit, and my surprise, she responded by admitting to being cowardly and ashamed of how she had behaved. She apologized for hurting me.

A little crack opened in my heart and I agreed to meet with her. We set a date for lunch. I stood outside the Wild Rose Thai restaurant wearing a tough mask to hide my nerves and vulnerability. She was late. For a moment, I thought, *"Maybe she's standing me up just to add insult to injury."* Then I regained my sanity and reminded myself she wouldn't do that. Then I thought, *"Maybe I should stand her up!"* Once again, regaining sanity, I remembered that was not who I was. And then she was there.

We were both extremely nervous, making small talk as we ordered. I put up a fortress of distrust across the table between us. Finally, she opened up the topic at hand. There were tears in her eyes and her voice was thin as she apologized. Something incredible and profound broke open in me. It was as though a veil dropped and suddenly we were sitting three feet closer together. No longer did I see her at a distance, as someone who had hurt me. I saw her as I used to, as a sister, a dear friend. I saw her pain, her deep discomfort, and the bravery it took for her to open up before me, and I was flooded with a wave of compassion so powerful my entire countenance changed. I remembered our shared love for one another and the planet we worked to protect. I realized I didn't want her to hurt or feel guilty. I wanted to protect her. I *was* her.

From someplace I didn't know existed, feeling as though it wasn't even me speaking, I said, "You know, I really appreciate you coming here and the courage it took to do this. I want you to know that when I look back, given the situation and what you were likely being told by advisors, I'm not sure I wouldn't have done the same thing."

Her face melted in relief and she said, "Thank you for saying that." By now we were both in tears.

We hugged when we parted. I didn't know if the friendship would ever rebuild, but I did know I felt lighter and kinder and my heart opened a bit wider. Allowing myself to feel genuine compassion for her discomfort created a pathway for us to remember our shared humanity. It opened a doorway to forgiveness. I was surprised that after our meeting I felt stronger. I hadn't lost anything by "letting her off the hook"; in fact, I had gained a deep sense of strength and a knowing that I had taken a step forward in healing.

We often think forgiving makes us vulnerable, but actually it's what helps restore a sense of personal power. After all vulner*ability* is an ability.

Forgiveness is not so much something we cross off the list as it is a journey, a practice of choosing over and over again. I continued to hate and resent but I also continued to choose over and over again to become fully willing and as I did, the levels of forgiveness deepened.

Having experienced such profound hatred within myself, such a strong dark desire to hurt those who'd hurt me, forced me to face my own shadow and I began to understand that in some ways I was not so very different from my attackers. I, too, had been driven by ego and insecurity. I, too, wanted to hurt them, to see them fail, because some part of me believed it would make me more and better. Although uncomfortable, facing this aspect of myself, combined with the compassionate encounter with my former friend, allowed me to soften some to the pain and weakness we all show at times in the challenge of our shared humanity. I began to understand that most of the attacks weren't even really about me; the attackers simply knew not who they really were. At the time, neither did I.

I now believe our True Selves do not attack. It is only when we are under the influence of ego, when we feel insecure and unsafe, that we harm others. It is when ego is in the driver's seat that we most strongly attach to the need to view ourselves as victims and have others view us as having been harmed. At some level, all attacks are a cry for help.

It helps to remember that hurt people hurt people. Bullies aren't the strong ones. They are the ones so weak and insecure they believe harming others, tearing others down will make them feel stronger and better. Their attacks aren't even about the person they go after. One of the most effective ways I've found to shut down bullies is to say, "I am so sorry that you are in such pain that you believe hurting me will make you feel better. I genuinely hope you find healing and peace." In my experience this has worked every time to silence those making nasty comments.

Forgiveness isn't saying what they did was okay; it's saying "I'm taking my power back." It's saying "I am not going to waste any more of my time, energy, peace, or power thinking about or fretting over you and what you did. No matter what took place in the past, I am not your victim."

Forgiveness is choosing not to define ourselves by those who have hurt us. *A Course in Miracles* notes that, "The unforgiven is a voice that calls out from a past forevermore gone by," and it goes on to offer a beautiful exercise, a prayer actually. Think of the person you need to forgive and say, out loud:

I give you to the Holy Spirit as part of myself.

I know that you will be released, unless I want to use you to imprison myself.

In the name of my freedom, I choose your release, because I recognize we will be released together.

One of the deepest levels of forgiveness is reaching the point where you realize the harm attempted against you by another wasn't actually harm at all, but a gift, a chance to grow into the next phase of your ever-evolving True Self. As Joseph said to his jealous brothers who sold him into slavery, "You meant evil against me, but God meant it for good."

Strategies for Developing Forgiveness

☞ Take radical responsibility

Be deeply honest with yourself. Notice if you are resisting forgiveness in order to maintain your identity as a victim. This can be very subtle and very uncomfortable to face but doing so offers massive liberation. Remember, forgiveness isn't saying what they did was okay; it's saying you are choosing to move beyond it. True forgiveness brings a quiet sense of power, a subtle knowing that we have moved beyond limits inflicted by the past. You can't always control what another person does to you, but you can always take control of what you do with it.

The place to start is to be honest with yourself about whether or not you are holding onto blame, anger, or resentment due to victim mentality or the need to maintain some story about your past that you have attached to. This honesty and process is not for wimps. As Mahatma Gandhi said, "The weak can never forgive. Forgiveness is the attribute of the strong." Often it takes a hard, uncomfortable look at ourselves. The thing is to become genuinely willing. Sometimes that takes a long while, but the liberation and power are worth the wait.

☞ "Practice" forgiveness with the little stuff

One way to scale up to the really intense relationships and experiences that require forgiveness is to practice it in less demanding conditions. Choose to forgive and detach from the guy that cuts you off in traffic or the coworker who cuts you off mid-sentence. Ninety percent of the time their actions actually have nothing to do with you; they are just caught in their own pain and problems. The more you use these little incidents as classrooms to release and forgive, the more easily you'll be able to get there with the big stuff.

☞   Replace the grievance with something else

One way I've found to begin to loosen a knot of unforgiving is to go under the situation to see a broader picture of what might have caused a person's hurtful behavior. This often allows us to tap into the compassion for our shared human challenges. My relationship with my brother is a good example. I often feel harshly and inaccurately judged by him. One time, after once again being shocked by harsh words, I stepped back and viewed it less personally. I remembered how we had been raised to be competitive with one another. I remembered my father screaming belittling things when my little brother hadn't performed to the desired outcome, shouting, "Your sister should have been the boy. She'd be winning! You little wimp."

I remembered how my heart ached when I witnessed that and couldn't stop it. In that remembering, compassion, and even a little sadness replaced the knot of unforgiveness, hurt, and anger.

☞   Forgive again and again and again

In the more intense, prolonged, or baggage-ridden cases, forgiveness usually isn't a one-and-done experience. More often, it's a process, a series of repeated forgivings. You choose, you release, and then the person does some new hurtful thing, or something triggers the old wounded feelings, and bang! You're right back in bondage. Then? You choose again. And again.

When Peter asked Jesus how many times he should forgive someone who had sinned against him, asking, "Up to seven times?" Jesus responded, "I tell you not just seven, but seventy-seven times!" Feeling anger is part of being human; staying stuck there is being a prisoner.

☞   The Four-Fold Process

In the *Book of Forgiving*, the Tutus outline the four-fold process for forgiveness that was used in South Africa's Truth and Reconciliation Commission. I strongly recommend reading their entire book. In the meantime, here are the steps:

> ☞   Telling the story, naming what happened to us. This is a critical step in reclaiming our dignity and making meaning of our hurting. There are many ways to do this and many choices in choosing with whom to share your story.
>
> ☞   Naming the hurt. This means being truthful about the pain of what happened to us. Feeling the pain helps us move to anger, and then to grief, and then to healing.
>
> ☞   Granting forgiveness. This is how we move from victim to hero, shifting from someone weak and at the mercy of others, to someone

who determines his or her own fate. Often, we cannot choose what happens to us, but we can choose what we do next. It means not carrying that person with you anymore.

☞ Renewing or releasing the relationship. Renewing is not returning to the way things were but instead creating a new relationship out of the suffering and it requires account-ability from both parties. And forgiving doesn't necessarily mean choosing to stay in a relationship. Sometimes staying would cause further harm. Sometimes the person has died or you don't know who it was that harmed you. This is when it makes sense to release that relationship.

One other aspect of releasing is letting go of those who continue to pity you, or stay focused on your wounds. If they cannot make the switch to seeing the glories with you, the beauty of your overcoming, let them go. Forgive them their attachment to your trauma and let both go.

At the time of this writing, four years after the onset of my ordeal, I have not mastered forgiveness but I have made, and am making, incredible progress and the journey is trans-forming and empowering every aspect of my life. In my coaching work I have not yet had a client come to me spe-cifically asking for help with forgiveness but very, very often, working with forgiveness becomes a key component to the breakthrough and progress my clients are seeking to achieve.

The odyssey of forgiving those we feel hurt or betrayed by can be one of the most profound and liberating journeys of our lives. It also holds the power to transform our world. *A Course in Miracles* notes that, "The holiest of all the spots on earth is where an ancient hatred had become a present love."

Forgiveness is healing. Forgiveness is holy ground. Forgiveness is freedom. Your release is up to you.

CHAPTER 6

Forgive Yourself

*"Never forget that to forgive yourself is to
release trapped energy that could be doing
good work in the world."*

—D. Patrick Miller

Forgiving others is just the tip of the iceberg. Deeper and often more difficult is the work of forgiving ourselves.

Just two weeks into the public shaming, John and I headed to southern Oregon for campaign events. We stayed with some old friends of John's on their beautiful ranch alongside the sparkling Umpqua River. The ranch stretches up from the river and flows out over rolling hills covered in hayfields, a small vineyard, native grassland, and oak groves. I had been there many times and loved the place, but this time I was nervous. These were long-standing friends and supporters of John. I was embarrassed and worried that they would blame me for having brought this mess into John's life and feared I would not be able to check my tears. I didn't want to face them, but I knew these people and this place were important to, and comforting for, John.

The first half hour or so was tortuous. We were all seated in their lovely rustic yet posh, ultra-modern kitchen. John and I were seated on stools along one side of the large square kitchen island as our hosts bustled around preparing dinner. I was aware of the conversation buzzing along but was so stressed and uncomfortable it was as though I was wrapped in cellophane, able to see and hear only blurrily, through layers from a distance.

Finally, Jane asked how I was doing, cutting right through the layers and snapping me back to the room. I looked at her and as I feared, felt the tears well up. She said, "Well, we don't have to talk about that right now," and just went about things in the kitchen like usual and normal. I wanted to flee.

A dark fog of shame, despair, and depression enveloped me. John sensed my anguish, asking several times what was wrong. Very uncharacteristically I just shook my head and brushed him off. I didn't think I could talk about it just then and make it through dinner.

However, not long after, before I realized what was happening, we did start talking about it. I expressed my sorrow and distress over not having told John about the marriage and making such a mess of the campaign. They listened and added stories and cursed the media. Jim said, "Well, you're headlong into something that most of us can't even imagine." They were completely non-judgmental, warm, and casual about it all. As I realized that they were not going to blame me or cast me out, the fog of distress thinned and my self-flagellation eased. I was indescribably grateful for their gentle kindness and acceptance.

That night, John and I slept in the lovely guest log cabin set into oak and pine trees overlooking the river. We had a quiet evening together and drifted off to much-needed sleep. It was not to last.

Prior to the bomb going off in my life, I had not kept my phone near my bedside, nor had I felt a stab of fear every time a call came in. At 3 a.m., it rang. I jolted awake. John blurted groggily, "Who is it?" It was a number I did not recognize.

I said, "I don't know, likely a wrong number." But to myself, I thought, *or perhaps a reporter whose number I don't know?* The damage was done. My gut clenched as I played out possible ugly implications of an unknown phone number.

On the heels of the anonymous phone call, Tessa, the ninety-five-pound lapdog, crawled up onto the bed, jiggling and jostling it like an earthquake. John could not get back to sleep. At 5 a.m. he gave up and bailed out. He sounded so horrendously exhausted. I felt terrible about the phone, the dog, all the damage I'd caused, all the mess I'd brought into his life, terrible about it all.

Guilt is too thin a word to describe what I experienced in the first months of my ordeal. The wreckage caused by my mistake was huge. Every day I faced the terrible reality of the damage done to work I cared so much about, the upheaval in state government, even the impact on my mother. But the worst was what it did to John. That changed everything, including Oregon history, and did more harm to the person I loved most in the world than anything else he'd ever faced.

As I noted earlier, John won reelection despite my mess, but the media and political opponents continued to hound him to resign. In an unprecedented move, the *Oregonian* editorial board demanded his resignation despite the fact that due process had not yet come close to determining if the allegations against us held water. The governor's top staff and campaign advisors just seemed to collapse after this. They were acting as though the mob was at the gate when it really was just a few media outlets.

The chief of staff and several political advisors asked to meet with us. They said the purpose of the meeting was to figure out how to get a handle on the media and strategize next steps, but as would be revealed, that wasn't really their intention. At 5:30 p.m., seven of us met at Mahonia Hall, gathering in the formal dining room, arrayed around the long, lacquered dark wood table. All but one political consultant looked exhausted.

Mahonia Hall is old and grand. It sits high on a forested hillside in a way that gives the impression of living in the canopy of the large maple and Douglas fir trees. That evening, in one of those real-life scenes an Academy Award-winning director couldn't have scripted any better, clouds began to amass in the sky outside the tall two-story windows and shortly after we sat down, lightning started to flash.

While thunder pealed and lightning crackled, we began to discuss the situation. To my absolute shock, they suggested John should resign. They had clearly discussed it prior to the meeting. I looked around the table at each of them and said, "Are you telling me it is inevitable that he resign? You are really going to give the *Oregonian* that much power, even though we haven't done what they've accused us of?" I looked at John and said, "Remember, the public didn't elect the *Oregonian* editorial board; they elected you. I think this is a terrible decision. At least take some time with it." None of his advisors said a word.

The meeting broke up with a heavy, heavy air; the darkness in the room mirrored the thick, dark clouds outside. I could sense this team knew it was over and I scribbled in my journal, "*I can't believe it. The fuckers are going to win. I can't believe I helped cause this.*"

I also couldn't believe John was going along with their suggestion. Numb with guilt and stress, I didn't know what to say but I did know his resigning would take a devastating toll on him. I desperately wanted to save him from the pain of second-guessing a terrible mistake. As he struggled with what to do, with his advisors saying he needed to move quickly, I said, "Dearest, you are the most meticulous, thorough decision-maker I've ever known, to the point it drives me crazy sometimes. Resignation is one of the biggest decisions you'll ever make. Surely it merits some time." He agreed and seemed to calm down a bit.

But it was not to be. The next several days were filled with Machiavellian maneuvering by the speaker of the house, the senate president, and the secretary of state, who was next in line for the governorship. Political opponents, including other Democratic leaders and climbers, turned on John, calling for his resignation. Smelling blood in the water, opportunists and the media pounced. I literally *was* the entire content of the main section of the *Oregonian*.

Reporters and photographers surrounded John's personal Portland home, my home in Bend, and Mahonia Hall. Up until that point I had managed to keep the media in the dark about my whereabouts. I was told that Good Morning America had reported I was still in Europe. Eventually they even sent helicopters to monitor John's home and CNN ran a segment, "Cops gather outside Kitzhaber House." They didn't point out they were there for John's protection, not for arrest. I spoke with John via phone several times during those terrible hours and he was extremely stressed. He said his house and neighborhood felt like a war zone. He was intensely worried about the impact it all was having on his son.

On February 13, I awoke around 4 a.m. at Mahonia, too stressed and guilt-laden to go back to sleep. That day my beloved life partner would resign and I knew in that moment the person I loved most in the world would make a decision that would eat him alive, and it was all due to my mistakes and reckless naiveté.

There is much, much more to John's story of having been the most successful politician in Oregon history and then being forced out, maligned, and losing so, so much. But that is his story to tell. All that I will share is that while I had already faced a good deal of serious adversity in my life, this was John's first. At times I really thought it might break him. Over the months as I began to heal, my greatest source of pain became watching him struggle with how to reconcile what had happened with his lifelong goals and dreams.

I did what I could to shore him up and boost his spirits and tried to give his mostly unspoken grief a gentle resting place. I also stayed very committed to my inner work and to regaining and maintaining my own balance so as to be better support for him. I used every technique I share in this book and then some to move through my own process of self-forgiveness.

The hard truth is that sometimes our mistakes make a mess of our lives and sometimes they take a terrible toll on those we love. Sometimes others do terrible things to us. We condemn ourselves for what we've done and sometimes for what has happened to us. Self-condemnation is a soul killer and one of the biggest limitations we place on ourselves; failing to forgive ourselves keeps us imprisoned in the past.

Humans screw up, period, every last one of us, and while we can't go back and undo most of it, beating ourselves up is the worst possible choice. Making a mistake, doing a bad thing, doesn't make us bad people. Really understanding that mistakes are a universal part of the human experience and that a bad action doesn't equate to a bad person is key to self-forgiveness and to forgiving others.

Moving past the harmful things we've done to others is only one aspect of self-forgiveness. The other is letting go of self-condemnation for the things we do to ourselves—the thoughts, habits, and behaviors we don't feel good about, that we're ashamed of. The drinking too much, eating too much, lusting too much, spending too much, exercising too little, and on and on. We can hide this stuff from others but never from ourselves and if we aren't careful, the inner shame we feel can erode us from the inside out.

Certainly any habit that leaves us with a sense of shame or feeling like we aren't living up to our full potential should be faced head-on. Most of these are worth letting go, even if that requires hard work and professional help. After all, feeling respected by others is nice, but feeling respect for ourselves is crucial. In order to fully love and respect ourselves, we need to be operating in integrity.

Addressing self-destructive habits is the subject of countless other books. The point I want to stress here is the importance of dropping self-condemnation even for the behaviors we aren't proud of. Harsh self-judgment is as crippling as unnecessary fear and can perpetuate the very behaviors we want to change. It keeps us feeling unworthy and not good enough and surely, there are already enough prompts to play those tapes. Lack of self-forgiveness blocks us from achieving our deepest longings and dreams. We all do things we'd rather not have the whole world see, but the less we allow those behaviors to define us, the more easily we can let them slide away.

As we strive to drop limiting behaviors, it's important to keep reminding ourselves that we are, at the core, good and worthy of good. We are human, and I don't mean that in the sense of merely human, lowly, flawed beings, but human as in beautiful, powerful, complex spiritual beings capable of greatness no matter how many times we forget it and screw up. The more we remember who and what we really are, the less there will be that seems to need forgiveness.

A Course in Miracles reminds, "How lovely does the world become in just that single instant when you see the truth about yourself reflected there. … Now you are holy and perceive it so."

Forgiveness is a two-way affair. If we want to help heal the wounds we've caused and be healed of wounds inflicted on us, we have to learn to forgive others *and* ourselves. One of the beautiful things about forgiving a fellow human being is that when we realize another person deserves forgiveness, we open a bit more to being able to accept that we, too, are worthy of forgiveness. Standing strong for yourself, in compassion, is essential to being genuinely strong and compassionate for others and essential to remembering your fully empowered Self.

Of all the relationships in life, the most important is the one with our Self. In those truly terrifying or beautifully ecstatic moments, no matter how much help, support, and encouragement we receive from friends and loved ones, at the end of the day, how it affects us is an inside job. We all deserve forgiveness. We all have goodness in us. We deserve to be our own best friend, to like the company we keep when no one else is near. After all, though finding happiness within may not be easy, finding it without is impossible.

Strategies for Self-Forgiveness

☞   Ask for forgiveness

In the early weeks, I was consumed by guilt about the damage my mistake was doing to John. During a session, I was sharing this my therapist when she asked, "Have you asked him for forgiveness?"

I said, "Yes, I've apologized many times."

She said, "But have you specifically asked forgiveness?"

Huh? Well, no. I hadn't.

Oddly, it took me two days to overcome the discomfort and muster the means.

John very candidly said, "You know, Cylvia, I still wish you could have trusted me enough to share this with me and if you hadn't stepped up to responsibility for the pieces of this that were your mistake, I'm not sure I would be able to, but yes, I do forgive you." I was surprised how much it eased my discomfort to hear him say so.

If you have harmed someone, even by mistake, ask their forgiveness. In most cases, living with the guilt is far worse than going to the person, confessing, and asking to be forgiven. Even if that person withholds forgiveness, there is healing in asking. Their choice not to forgive is not your business, burden, or poison to drink.

☞   Make amends

If you have done something dishonest or harmful, you know it. If you can do anything to remediate the damage, do it. If you've stolen money, repay it. If you've said something cutting, apologize and explain that it was more about you than the person you attacked. As hard as it is to step up in honesty to the harm we do to others, it is absolutely worth it. There is no replacement for self-respect.

Sometimes making amends means paying it forward. As I moved through my healing process, I became painfully aware of how much I wished I had been kinder and more supportive of my sister while she was alive. My therapist suggested I write a love letter to her. As I was meditating and thinking about this, I realized that the best way I could offer love to my sister was to continue to support and guide her kids; my nephew and niece. I stepped into that role with increased commitment and intention. Helping those young people heal and establish beautiful lives is my ultimate love letter to my sister. I feel her smiling even as I type this.

I love you, sis, and I miss you. Thank you for everything you did for me.

Self-forgiveness is not a free pass. It requires a truly honest, sometimes painfully honest, look at ourselves, our actions, and their consequences. It requires a genuine desire to correct what can be corrected, learn from our mistake, and choose not to repeat it. True self-forgiveness requires a desire to change. The liberation is absolutely worth the discomfort.

☞ Place your guilt on someone else

Imagine someone else in your place doing the thing you did. Put yourself in a place of judgment and write out how you think that person should be punished or shown mercy. Chances are you would not punish them nearly as harshly as you might punish yourself. Usually the judgment we heap on ourselves is far, far harsher than what we would heap on others for the same habits and behaviors.

☞   Be vigilant with your language to and about yourself

One habit to pay attention to is how we talk to and about ourselves. I'm often shocked by the way people talk to themselves. Self-deprecation is a device we use to fit in, or to be funny, or to not come across as too full of ourselves. We treat it as though it's benign; it isn't. The more we tell ourselves something, the more likely it is to settle in as a core belief. I am learning to be much more vigilant in how I choose to talk to about myself. When I make a mistake, I say, "Well, Cyl, you'll do that one better next time." When I find that I've slipped into a limiting or lazy old habit and I find myself feeling less than my best, I say, "Okay, that might have been a waste of time and mind, but now I'm choosing better."

I also notice moments to give myself an out-loud verbal pat on the back. When I make it through a workout even though I really wanted to skip that day, I say, "Good job, Self!"

One day at the gym recently I did just that and a woman overheard and said, "Wow, what a nice way to talk to yourself. I'm going to do the same thing!" Absolutely! Celebrate yourself, sister!

The other piece of self-talk is how we describe ourselves to others. Be careful of the labels you attach to yourself. You are not what you did or didn't do. You aren't what was done to you. No one is a thief, a liar, an offender. We are human beings who sometimes forget our own goodness and do things that hurt others, sometimes even terrible things. The act is not the being we are unless we choose to keep doing it. Similarly, no one is just a survivor unless she chooses to stop there. Be careful to avoid choosing a self-description that keeps you trapped someplace you don't really want to be.

Pay attention to how you're talking to yourself, out loud or internally. Would you talk that way to your best friend, your sister, or anyone? Then don't say it to yourself! Similarly, are you doing things that you would compliment someone else for? Then give yourself a little of that same recognition and praise.

A lot of the self-help work we do is counterproductive. With the best of intentions we work to improve ourselves, get rid of aspects we don't like, and overcome personal shortcomings. And all the while this focus on fixin' what's wrong with us just reinforces the message that there's something fundamentally wrong with us!

I had spent most of my adult life trying to do an exorcism on that part of me that struggled with money. That issue surged back up in a big way during my long deconstruction and reconstruction period. A while back I was taking one of the Unity ministerial pre-req classes called Self Awareness. It was being taught by my home minister, Jane Hiatt, and one of the books she had us study was *Conscious Living*, by Gay Hendricks.

Between the reading and her teaching, a lightbulb went off for me. I realized that had it not been for the challenges I'd had (or perceived I'd had, anyway) around money, I never would have gone as deep in developing my talents or my spiritual growth. I had been pretty darned successful in many other areas and I think had I not had to work through the nuisance of the scarcity belief aspect of myself, I just wouldn't have put so much effort into growing. That part of myself that I'd been loathing had actually been critical to becoming the best I could be. Once this settled in, I thanked that part of me for its service, gave it genuine appreciation, and let it know it was no longer needed.

Forgiving others helps us stop giving away our power. Forgiving ourselves opens us up to the possibility that our true power is beyond anything we'd ever imagined.

At some point in my journey of self-forgiveness, I came across this poem by Galway Kinnell.

Saint Francis and the Sow
The bud
stands for all things,
even those that don't flower,
for everything flowers, from within, of self-blessing;
though sometimes it is necessary
to reteach a thing its loveliness,
to put a hand on its brow
of the flower
and retell it in words and touch
it is lovely
until it flowers again from within, of self-blessing;
as Saint Francis
put his hand on the creased forehead
of the sow, and told her in words and in touch
blessings of earth on the sow, and the sow
began remembering all down her thick length,
from the earthen snout all the way
through the fodder and slops to the spiritual curl of the tail,
from the hard spininess spiked out from the spine
down through the great broken heart

to the sheer blue milken dreaminess spurting and shuddering
from the fourteen teats into the fourteen mouths sucking and
blowing beneath them:
the long, perfect loveliness of sow.

We are learning and growing; journeying. Mistakes will happen. We will stumble along the way. And still, no matter our past, no matter the mistakes, no matter what others may think they see, we each are unique, good, and beautiful. We all deserve to show ourselves some grace and kindness, to place our hand upon our own brow and remind ourselves of our own perfect loveliness.

CHAPTER 7

Give

*"I have found that among its other benefits,
giving liberates the soul of the giver."*

—*Maya Angelou*

Immediately upon John's resignation we had to move our things out of Mahonia Hall while dealing with the ongoing barrage of media coverage and onlookers. I packed up while a throng of reporters paced and peered from just outside the front gates. I literally ran around the house moving things and piling up boxes, working up a sweat and ducking past windows, determined to keep the media guessing about my whereabouts.

I returned to my Bend home and spent the next two weeks unpacking while trying to dodge the reporters and photographers who circled my house like vultures and voyeurs. Given that my home was small and I liked to park my car inside the one-car garage, old things had to be cleared out in order for me to move new things in. John and I borrowed my neighbors' truck and, when there was a gap in gawking reporters, ran a load of stuff to Goodwill and then took an old, worn-out box spring and a whole load of old assorted campaign signs to the dump.

It wasn't a smart move. Someone recognized us and called the police to come and sort through the trash we had dumped. Unbelievably, they also called the media. As a result we were next trashed in a sensationalist story about our trash. Again, no smoking guns, nothing glamorous, no shady documents in our trash.

On another day, I was out in my garage, unpacking boxes, with the garage door open. A car slowly circled the cul de sac; the man inside stared at me. I closed the garage door and pulled the blinds in the house. Sixty seconds later, a photographer showed up. I watched from behind the blinds as he stalked around the front of my home.

Later still, I was lying on my couch feeling depressed and overwhelmed by the whole thing. The woodstove had overheated the place so I opened the front window just in time to hear people talking outside, and someone asking my dear friend and neighbor about me. I got up, pulled the shade, and slipped around to the side of the window as another reporter and cameraman came all the way to my front door and rang the bell. It rattled me because I hadn't realized they could come to the front door. If I hadn't opened the window in time to overhear them, he would have wound up looking right in my front window at me lying on my couch. I felt hunted.

I also felt valueless. I had no job, no clients. All the volunteer work I'd been doing as First Lady was gone. As devastated as I was, I wanted, needed even, to find a way to be of use, of service, to someone beyond myself, so I started volunteering.

I put old skills to use and helped out at an injured wildlife rehabilitation facility and got involved with Fences for Fido, an organization that builds fences for dogs that are living chained up. I had learned about Fences for Fido while serving as First Lady, but had been far too busy to personally participate; with my career being off the rails, I suddenly had plenty of time.

The second building project really hooked me. A team of volunteers built a fence for three dogs living on short, thick chains. One, a super friendly Chow mix, had his huge chain so tightly wound he could only move about three feet in any direction. When the fence was up and we cut the chain off, he ran around for the first minute or so like a prancing horse, with his front legs high in the air. He had become so accustomed to wearing the huge heavy chain, he had to relearn how to walk. Soon his gait normalized and he was running easily, sniffing his new digs, panting, grinning. His joyous exuberance loosened the chains of loss around my own heart. At least I had made a difference for somebody that day. I hadn't just fixated on and marinated in my own brokenness; I'd gone out and made one life a little better. In giving, I'd received.

More than anything else, my identity destruction and reconfiguration experience was a journey of spiritual growth and awakening. As that journey progressed, it, too, became a way of giving to others, even if unintentionally. As part of my own healing, I was taking quite a few courses through Unity. At some point I decided I might as well enroll in the ministerial program so that I could at least be getting official credit for courses I was taking anyway. Soon I was being asked to deliver a few Sunday talks and serve on a couple of committees at my local congregation.

The work I was doing with *A Course in Miracles* was so powerful and challenging to long-held misbeliefs that I longed to have others to discuss it with, so I started up a study group. A dozen people came to the first meeting. Over time it dwindled down to a group of four women who went through deep transformation together, learned a common language from the *Course,* and became cherished, lifelong friends.

I still lacked an outlet for my environmental work and that was unsettling, but I filled a little gap there when I helped launch an environmental sustainability program at the local Unity and sometime later was elected to the Unity Worldwide EarthCare team.

I still had no idea what was going to take place with my career or how I would ever climb out from under the ongoing hatchet-job attacks from the *Oregonian* and *Willamette Week*, but I did know it felt good, and healthy, to be doing something of value for others, even in the midst of my own challenges and uncertainty. In addition to giving me a sense of doing something of value, volunteering turned out to be an important social connection. Most of the other volunteers didn't know who I was and those who did were kind and supportive. It was a small but important step in reclaiming a place in community.

One of the biggest lessons I learned in my dark night of the soul was that while we're navigating this mysterious, magnificent, not-for-wimps human experience, sometimes the biggest contributions we make have nothing to do with causes or social movements but are found instead in how we choose to respond to the events life throws at us.

A year and a half into the ongoing life upheaval, I was out on my deck, writing, when John called. He was sobbing, barely able to speak. Then, finally, "Cyl, Logan's been in a head-on car wreck. They're airlifting him to the hospital."

My breath stopped. *Oh my God. What more? How much more can we take?* I put my head down on the table. With sickness in the pit of my stomach came the thought, *This might finally break him. If his son doesn't survive, I'm not sure John will."*

Logan did survive. His recovery, however, required massive physical caretaking, and time and expense navigating the legal implications. I worried that the added burden would wear John even thinner and maybe even break him. But the beautiful truth was, it had just the opposite effect. John's grief and angst over the investigations and the loss of his work was partially overridden by the deep love for his son and his determination to provide healing and support. It gave him a new focus and he was far less rudderless and depressed. For a time, the seeming tragedy gave John renewed purpose and in the end it helped him move past the loss and trauma and toward healing. It also launched our young man on a powerful journey of personal growth and health.

The seemingly terrible event gifted me with something—an even deeper respect for and appreciation of my mate. He didn't break, even under pain and pressure that would have destroyed many. There is a beautiful poem called *The Invitation*, by Oriah Mountain Dreamer. In it is a line that reads:

It doesn't interest me to know where you live or how much money you have. I want to know if you can get up, after the night of grief and despair, weary and bruised to the bone, and do what needs to be done to feed the children."

That is exactly what John Kitzhaber did over and over and over again. Witnessing the power of his love was awe-inspiring and it became a powerful example for me many, many months later, when I brought my nephew home and my own parenting began in earnest.

With the wisdom of hindsight, I now see that I did in fact make a tremendous contribution during those years I was sidelined from my professional path. Through those many, many months of deep uncertainty, I was there for John, offering support, suggestions, insights at times, love at all times, encouraging him in his own healing, reinvention, and reemergence. I was there for my sister's son, my son, really, as he navigated building a new life. I was there increasingly for my mom as she opened her heart and home to my niece and great-niece, and then to a boyfriend and then a new baby. Mom amazed and inspired me with her ability to expand love and embrace flexibility as she headed into her eighties and I was so grateful to be of some support as she did so.

And, of course, through it all, I was there for my beloved dog Tessa, making sure she had the best love and care even during those stretches when I just wanted to fold in on myself.

Looking back, those exercises of love may have saved my life. Looking forward, extending love to others, may be the biggest contribution I ever make in this lifetime. Learning to be more generous with love is a tremendous gift to ourselves and we are never valueless when we are easing the pain and the progress of others.

Sometimes those moments when we feel we have the least to give are the moments when giving back is the most important and valuable thing we can do. When we've lost the career, the partner, the role that we had attached our sense of importance and worth to, giving to others can become a tremendous gift to ourselves.

Strategies for Giving, Receiving, and Remembering Your Value

☞ Volunteer for a cause you care about

When we're facing intense challenges in our own lives, it may seem counterintuitive to focus on giving to someone else but it can be one of the most healing and empowering actions we can take. Volunteering helps shift focus away from the problem and even from our own pain and helps us remember we still have value and something to contribute even when aspects of our lives may seem out of control. Sometimes volunteering uncovers skills and talents we didn't know we had or leads to beautiful new friendships. The volunteer position doesn't have to be big in scope or feel like a part-time job. Just find something to help another, especially something that has immediate benefits to another life. As Mother Theresa said, "It's not how much we give but how much love we put into giving."

☞   BUT, put your own oxygen mask on first!

As cliché as it sounds, we're only really able to serve others when we take care of ourselves. I knew the best way I could support John was to stay committed to my own healing so that I could be balanced and grounded when he had moments of grief and wavering. Prioritizing time for meditation, spiritual work, and counseling as needed was the equivalent of putting my own oxygen mask on first so that I could help him breathe through the suffocating, oppressive turbulence that was the backdrop of our lives at that time.

Our modern culture has carried a strong message that self-care is selfish. Many of us have bought into the belief that sacrifice and burnout are required to be of value and of service. This is an illusion. If you want to do your best for others, you must do well for yourself. Otherwise you are playing the victim and actually are not giving the other person, or cause, the best you have to offer.

☞   Don't underestimate simple love and kindness

Sometimes the most valuable, healing form of giving is simple human kindness and love. A few weeks into my public shaming, when the media was crazed and the stress levels enormous, but before John had resigned from office, early one morning I made my way, wrapped in the dirty bathrobe I'd lived in for days, down to the kitchen. I was feeling unbelievably low, guilty, and unworthy.

John was sitting on the counter next to the sink. He reached over and pulled me into a hug and said, "You are lovely, Cylvia. You are a lovely human being ... But that is the filthiest housecoat I think I've ever seen." I looked down at my once- white robe, now gray and marked with orange splotches of spaghetti sauce, yellow beer stains, and God only knew what else. I started to laugh. He laughed too. My spirit lightened in the warmth of his love and in the laughter and I found the strength to pick myself up, get some exercise, and do a much-needed load of laundry.

Before all of the big mess happened, John and I had been together for ten years and we had never raised our voices or said an intentionally hurtful thing to one another. Amazingly, after all of this, all that we've been through, I can still say that's the case. Gratitude is too small a word for what I feel for and about this beautiful relationship.

Throughout our long challenge we were unfailingly kind to one another and that likely is what saved our relationship. Many, many others were kind to us, in ways big and small, and, during our darkest moments, those acts of simple kindness may have saved our lives. One of the best ways to turn our tragedies into triumph is to allow ourselves to become kinder, more empathetic, and compassionate when we witness our fellow beings facing life's hardships. This simple choice can save a life and heal our world.

Even in our most broken moments we have opportunities to give. No matter what or how much we've lost, we can always do something for someone else. Offering value, comfort, or love to others is a powerful way to clear the rubble and debris from the tragedies that blow holes in our expectations of what life should be. Giving to others is a step toward remembering our value when we're questioning ourselves, and of shifting focus off the losses and back onto our many skills and talents. Being a source of help and support to someone else can help us remember that we are a part of, and also supported by a vast matrix of people who make everything in our lives possible. Easing another being's suffering always eases our own, and giving always is receiving.

In this materialistically insane society, we are so often fed the message that giving involves losing something—our money, possessions, time, whatever—that we are trained to believe that giving things away diminishes our own supply. When it comes to love and kindness, that is pure BS. Albert Schweitzer once wrote:

> *Our humanity is by no means so materialistic as foolish talk is continuously asserting it to be ... I am convinced that there is far more in [people] of idealist will power than ever comes to the surface of the world. Just as the water of the streams we see is small in amount, compared to that which flows underground, so the idealism which becomes visible is small in amount, compared to what men and women bear locked in their hearts...*

The world is thirsty for love and kindness. The more we allow our full volume of these to surface and flow, the more we feel in return and the more readily we expand into our True Selves. Giving and receiving are one.

CHAPTER 8

Reframe the Story Reclaim Your Power

"The lens we view experiences through shapes our reality more than the experiences themselves."

—*Cylvia Hayes*

The way we choose to view the events of our lives shapes our lives more than the events themselves.

Losing the career I had spent twenty-five years building was a rib-breaking body blow. My work wasn't just a job; it was my mission. I have a deep, profound, very personal love for nature and the myriad species we share this planet with. In my early twenties, I learned about how we were hemorrhaging species and wild places due to relentless human consumption and unsustainable business and economic models. This lit a fire under me to do what I could to help humanity develop a healthier, less destructive, more restorative relationship with the rest of nature. I'd been working toward that aim ever since as an advocate, activist, consultant, business owner, government worker, and as First Lady of Oregon.

Before the public shaming, after nearly twenty years of work in my field, I had just reached the place where I had become one of the national leaders in the new economy and climate action movements. I found myself keynoting at events with people in the audience whom I had studied under.

And then, in one blinding flash, it was gone. Agony. My ego raged. The identity I had created, the self I believed myself to be, was utterly dependent upon my work and it was brutal having it torn away. *Who was I if I wasn't that? If that could be so easily taken away, had I ever really been of any value or importance at all?* My doings and busyness had shielded me from truly facing those terrifying questions.

At first, in an effort to stave off the deep, lonely, and uncomfortable work of facing what I truly believed about myself, my value or lack-thereof, and out of fear of not being able to pay my bills, I railed and hustled and tried to keep my work alive. I got a client here and there after the first few months but I didn't do my best work. In desperation, I took on a client that I knew looked like trouble, and sure enough, a few months in, I got stiffed for several thousand dollars, something that had never before happened in my professional career.

Meanwhile the amount of time it was taking to work through the legal implications of the false allegations against me was almost incalculable. Meetings and calls with attorneys, poring over reams of documents and materials, writing public statements in response to the ongoing media assaults. It was, literally, an unpaid half- to full-time job for months on end and I hated it and resented having to spend precious time doing it. Patience had never been my strong suit and I was intensely frustrated with the process that had been thrust upon me. But there was no escaping the legal mess. I knew that the time I was putting into it paled in comparison to the time my team of public defense attorneys was spending on it, so I did what I could to hold up my end and do the job at hand.

As I forced myself forward in the legal processes, the media attacks kept coming and my exhaustion deepened. Finally I had to face the fact that I was too broken to go on pushing my work like a river up a mountain. I knew I needed to give in to the exhaustion and the circumstances and accept that it was going to be a long time before I'd be able to work in my field again, but I didn't really know how to do it.

Finding a way to give myself permission was the next step on my journey of gaining better control of my mind. I had been viewing what had happened to me and the disruption in my work as being taken out, defeated by powerful enemies. Just giving in to that was beyond my surrender capacity. And then I had a breakthrough; I began to consider that maybe there was another way of looking at the situation. Yes, it was true I'd been sidelined against my will. On the other hand, I'd also been given a lot of free time, space for inner work, therapy, healing, and even doing art, which I hadn't done in thirty years. Right then I made the decision to reframe and view the situation as an unasked for sabbatical.

As soon I did, something amazing happened; I liked it! I liked not being so driven, so busy all the time. I liked having hours to read, to soak, to take long walks, and even just lie on the couch and watch television. And I loved devoting my bruised and weary self to the inner journey and spiritual development—long meditations, journaling, reading, reflecting, studying, taking a few courses. I stopped working and opened up to being worked on. Thus began my quest of questioning and the blessed discipline of becoming aware of my thoughts and those oft-repeated thoughts I'd let gel into beliefs.

The more I became aware of my thoughts, the more I started to notice the stories I told myself. We are a storytelling species. The stories we tell others help us communicate, educate, entertain, and connect. The stories we tell ourselves shape the kind of life we're going to have. No matter how terrible the situation we may be facing, there are many angles to it, and many stories we can believe about it; the story we choose will either undermine or empower our ability to respond.

The beliefs we hold literally control our lives and how we experience ourselves, others, and life itself. And the stories we tell ourselves reveal beliefs that we often aren't aware of but that are running our lives.

Certain thoughts tend to grab us more powerfully than others and they are aggressive for attention. Thoughts we focus on over and over form beliefs, whether or not they are actually true. As we're locking into beliefs, we're also discovering and creating stories about the world and ourselves. These stories both reflect and strengthen our beliefs, both conscious and hidden. They narrow down the options we can see for handling life events and narrow our perception of ourselves to a fraction of what we truly are.

Reframing how we choose to view a challenging situation helps us reclaim some power and open up to possible solutions we might not see otherwise. My decision to reframe my situation as a sabbatical opened new ways of viewing a number of entrenched old stories. Financial scarcity, or at least the fears around it, had been a lifelong challenge for me. I had just started making really good money and paid off all debts except my mortgage before John ran for office again. I had grown a successful consulting business, traveled to nearly twenty countries, run for office, and served as First Lady of Oregon living in a mansion, and yet, there I was, once again scrambling to pay my bills and stressed out about money.

Taking a sabbatical didn't really seem financially possible. I had stopped taking paid work at the beginning of 2014 so that I could really harness the First Lady position to make change. John and I had never blended our finances or even checking accounts. I had no savings. But I did have faith and a growing sense that I was in the midst of profound and purposeful growth.

All my adult life, people had referred to me as resourceful. It made me cringe because I interpreted it as having been capable and creative because I had to be, because I hadn't come from wealth, didn't have much family support, etc. But, I now knew there was another way of looking at it. I was certainly at a point where I was having income and cash-flow challenges, but I also had enormous resources flowing to me—unexpected support, even from surprising supporters. My neighbors were stepping up to provide maintenance on my house as needed. John was helping with my expenses even though he was dealing with his own massive legal fees. And as for that, I was receiving an enormous amount of free legal support. Not only did I have an all-star team of public defenders, but the high-priced top-caliber criminal defense attorneys stayed on my team pro bono. Even the skilled appellate attorney who took up my defense against the *Oregonian* did so at no cost to me.

I might have been struggling to pay my bills but I was receiving an inflow of support from friends and millions of dollars of free legal services. Even though it didn't look like I'd envisioned, I was, in fact, being abundantly supported. So, I decided to stop thinking about being forced to be resourceful and instead began focusing on the fact that I was resource-full.

I began to work in earnest on redirecting any fear related to money and telling myself a different story. I had a home equity line of credit and that kept things afloat for about six months; right after I'd maxed it out and didn't know how I was going to pay the next month's bills, I received a completely unexpected $14,000 check from a supporter, enough to keep things going several more months. It was an unfamiliar feeling of being supported by life in general, and it was altogether glorious.

The power of telling a different story applies to what's currently playing out in our lives as well as to our pasts. The stories we tell ourselves about the past have tremendous influence over how we live our lives in the present. They can either empower us or keep us chained to limitations, fears, and self-loathing.

Even though I appreciated many of the skills I'd gained from my early life, I had always viewed my rough childhood as a huge obstacle to overcome. I was proud of having risen out of family patterns and gotten a formal education, but some deep part of me feared that my lack of upper middle class history might hold me down. When John and I first started dating and interacting with his Ivy League peers, I was intimidated even though I pushed through it with forced confidence. The feeling of being cut from the wrong cloth intensified as I moved higher in political circles and was often surrounded by people from more affluent backgrounds and family legacies. And then, lo and behold, one of those affluent types dug into my crazy, unconventional past and used it to blow our lives to pieces.

At first, in the early weeks of despair and terror, I wondered if I'd been right all along, if it was indeed true that someone like me couldn't run in certain circles or succeed beyond certain levels. Over time, as I did the inner work, and my understanding and spiritual quickening rolled forward, I realized I had obviously made a huge mistake of naiveté but that didn't erase the intelligence, vision, hard work, and creativity that had allowed me to rise into the positions I'd been holding. I had lost those positions, but not the knowledge and talents that had made them possible in the first place.

As our ordeal dragged on, John and I were clearly in it together but in very different places and going through very different processes. His struggle is not my story to tell, but witnessing it gave me a different window frame through which to view my past. I began to realize that the unconventional, shall we say "colorful" history, was actually what had given me the resiliency muscle to become a first-generation college graduate, successful entrepreneur, and highly unconventional First Lady of Oregon.

There is no question I experienced some deep trauma as a child, but there was also real love, opportunities, and unusually rich experiences. As I came to better understand the difference between ego and True Self, I realized it was the victim mentality of ego that had caused me to cling so hard to a certain way of viewing my past.

The story I had always told was of being a tough scrapper, someone who had overcome an abusive family, who had gained success despite a rough upbringing. Through a certain lens, all of that was true, but I began to question whether that narrative was actually serving me. I began to wonder if my unconscious decision to wrap my identity so tightly around being someone who overcame hardship had perhaps generated more hardship! I had a strong notion that I had limited myself by leaning so hard on the story of a tough childhood and so I began to rewrite the story.

Allowing space for a different story about my past made room for a renewed and transformed relationship with my mother. I thought I had accepted the loss of a close relationship with my mother, but instead, I began to see I had embraced it because it kept alive the old story of hardship and abandonment upon which I'd built my identity. I had always been irritated with my mom because I felt she kept rewriting our history, putting a rosy glow on some seriously dark things, and failing to acknowledge what had really happened. But there in my own tremendous crisis I began to understand that Mom wasn't in denial; it wasn't that she didn't believe the dark things hadn't happened, but she had just made a conscious decision to choose happiness. I realized my old wounds and toughness identity had robbed her of my respect and both of us of a loving relationship for decades. The truth is my mother's living demonstration of resiliency and positivity in the face of tremendous hardship is one of the biggest privileges and advantages I have been given in this life.

The important point about our pasts is not what happened to us, but what we choose to do with it. One of the many gifts in my public shaming ordeal is that I had finally experienced enough adversity and suffered enough to let go of the old identity tied to toughness. I no longer wanted to fight my way through life; I wanted to love my way through. As the media and political opponents concocted an ugly public narrative about me, I took control of the narrative I'd been creating about myself.

At that point, with the swirl of arduous circumstances still blowing through my outer life, but deeply into the "sabbatical" of inner work, I was in a full-blown rethinking of how I had been thinking about everything and working to stay open to different approaches to every circumstance. Life dealt plenty of opportunities to practice.

In January 2018, I shattered my leg. The horse I was riding lost his footing, all four feet washed out from under him, and he fell down hard on his left side, right on top of me. He scrambled up, leaving me facedown in the dirt. I don't even remember rolling over, sitting up, and looking down at my legs. Even before my mind registered what I was seeing, I had a full-body sick feeling that something was seriously wrong. *Oh God. Oh no.* My left foot was bent out at a ghastly ninety-degree angle and the shinbone was trying to poke through the skin just above the ankle.

This wasn't my first rodeo with a serious orthopedic injury and I knew the pain was about to get really, really bad. I couldn't believe I was seriously injured again. My mind started down the path of, *Oh man, I can't afford this. I can't afford it financially, or the time off, or the disruption to everything I need to do.* But then, I shifted, made the choice not to judge the situation, and asked, *Maybe there is a different way to look at this. Maybe this is happening for me and not just to me. What do I want the outcomes to be?*

> *I want to be able to walk again.*
>
> *I want this to increase my spiritual awakening.*
>
> *I want it to empower my work.*
>
> *I want to have beautiful encounters with everyone I interact with in dealing with this.*

And then the mind-searing pain hit and there was no more thinking, just writhing, gasping, trying to keep breathing. There's a lot more to the whole story. Having the emergency room orthopedic surgeon look at the X-ray and say, "Wow. Oh my goodness." Getting knocked out on ketamine while my beloved John, former emergency room doc, helped the surgeon set my leg. Two days later, undergoing surgery that required twelve screws and two plates to piece back together more than twenty bone fragments. The terrible pain. Blah, blah, blah.

A bigger part of the story was how ego got me into the mess in the first place. I hadn't been riding in a couple of years and I really didn't want to go that day. But the invitation had come from a woman who had previously criticized me based on the media coverage. She reached out to apologize and I was moved and impressed with the courage it took to do so. So when she invited me to go riding, I agreed to meet her at her ranch.

I'm an experienced horsewoman and I knew the horse I was riding wasn't settled. Nonetheless, wanting to impress the woman, I put him into a gallop. The next thing I knew I was on the ground, the horse on top of me, and the woman I'd been trying to impress was calling the ambulance. I had literally let ego take the reins.

The even bigger and more important part of the story is how my reframe of the situation delivered miracles. As I noted above, before I went down the rat hole of freaking out I took a pause to consider that maybe it was happening for me to decide what I wanted the outcomes to be. As it turned out, I had incredible care from ambulance and emergency room responders, surgeons, nurses, therapists—I had deep conversations with some of them. I opened up and asked for help (a big, new thing for me) and had dozens of people bring me food, run errands, even clean my house while I was healing. The insurance companies stepped up to cover all of the costs and then some. Instead of viewing the broken leg as a problem, I viewed it as a project and a laboratory. I healed months ahead of schedule and, unlike what doctors said was likely, started running again.

Experiencing responding to my broken leg with such calm, assurance, and even joy allowed me to see how much I had grown, how much the learning I'd been undergoing the past few years had integrated into my being, and that built my confidence that maybe the whole terrible-seeming mess of the public shaming and the legal challenges, and even the financial challenges, might all actually be happening *for* me, for my good. What did I have to lose by asking that question?

As I allowed for the possibility that maybe it was all happening *for* me, the losses began to feel less like loss. For example, with a little distance from the immediate pain of so abruptly losing my public position, I realized I hadn't wanted most of it. I was glad to be rid of the constant busyness, glad not to have to spend time on tasks and events that I wasn't passionate about, glad not to have to split my time between my private home and the official governor's residence. I was glad to be back at the center of my own life.

Unlike what I'd first believed, my business wasn't lost. Yes, I had lost my clients and had my reputation smeared, but I still had a business license, name, history, systems, and work products. I opened up to the possibility of a different story, a different perspective; I shifted the lens, adjusted focus, and let in a bit more light.

There's a striking tale called the *Parable of the Three Stonecutters* made famous by renowned management consultant Peter Drucker:

> *A man came across three stonecutters and asked them what they were doing. The first replied, "I am making a living." The second kept on hammering while he said, "I am doing the best job of stonecutting in the*

entire county." The third looked up with a
visionary gleam in his eye and said, "I am
building a cathedral."

It's all about the lens we view things through and the story we tell.

We think we know when a thing is true or not, especially when it involves our suffering. Getting fired, divorced, or in a terrible car accident, or nailed by cancer—those are facts. But what is the full truth of each of those situations? How many times do we come out the other side of something that seemed truly terrible in the midst of it but turned out to be incredibly positive in hindsight? The trick is learning to stay open to that possibility even when the scene in front of us looks grim.

This is what I now know. We are not what we have lost. We are not what has been torn from us, and we definitely are not broken beyond repair, ever, unless we choose to build that brokenness and victimhood into our beliefs, our stories, and our identities. Even when it all blows to pieces, we still *are* everything we were before. We might not still *have* what we had—the positions, the possessions, money, the athletic body, the children, loved ones—but we still *are* the culmination of experiences, talents, and current and former abilities that make us uniquely us. Every one of us is the sum total of all we have experienced, felt, learned, and unlearned before. The shifting of jobs, homes, and the people in our lives opens opportunities to redirect our unique set of experiences, insights, and skills into powerful and positive new directions we might not otherwise have explored. There is never only one way to view a challenging event and there is never only one possible outcome.

Life is flow and ebb and ever-changing. It comes and goes and comes again and while some losses will always leave a gap, in each there is also potential for new addition and richness. When we stop clinging so hard to the old and familiar, we open ourselves to new and incredible possibilities we wouldn't have imagined.

The life cycle of the butterfly is truly a magical and exquisite gift unveiled on this planet. Suddenly, the little caterpillar is struck with an irresistible force of change. Once it has wrapped itself inside a chrysalis, its body literally begins to disintegrate. At some point, long-dormant cells called imaginal cells activate. At first, the old caterpillar body attacks them as foreign intruders, but the attacks just serve to hasten the disintegration. Finally, at a point of maximum destruction of the old form, the imaginal cells reach a critical mass and sort of wake up, recognize one another, and realize they are no longer a worm, but a winged butterfly. They tell themselves, and the world, a different story.

Life is like that. We can stay folded in, wrapped in the cocoon of loss, fight against the changes, and rail against the time it takes to put it all behind, or we can go deep enough, long enough to transform, break through old confines, unfurl with new depth and perspective, and fly. No matter how hard the situation, that choice is always ours and our story is ours to write, and to live.

Strategies for Empowered Reframing

☞   The Choose Again exercise

A Course in Miracles is a mind-bending spiritual approach to psychotherapy. One of the things I most appreciate about it is that it is both deeply, sometimes even disturbingly profound, and at the same time very practical. One of the tremendously useful practical techniques it recommends is to "Choose Again." This is a simple practice that will profoundly change your life.

It goes like this …

Each time you find yourself fixated on a fear of something beyond your control, or each time you find yourself obsessing about what someone did to you, or find yourself thinking negative thoughts about yourself, simply notice it, say "choose again," and think about something else, almost anything else.

Some days I had to do that five hundred times when obsessing over a particularly consuming or uncomfortable repetitive thought and sometimes the only positive thing I could think to focus on was the birdsong outside, the big dog beside me on the couch, or John's latest sweet little note of love and encouragement. Anything positive. It was work, and it took commitment, but eventually it always did the trick. As my thinking shifted, my lens adjusted, and my life improved.

Angry at your criticizer? Choose again. Resentful of your spouse? Choose again. Terrified about the "what ifs?" Choose again. Replaying the ugly scene over and again in your head? Choose again. This simple but profound tool helps put us in the driver's seat of our own mind and helps us become aware of thoughts that are causing unpleasant feelings.

Reframing works for really big catastrophic life events and also for everyday little things. A friend just canceled lunch at the last minute. Either it's a rude dismissal or it's the gift of an hour's free time you hadn't seen coming. Which feels better? We may not be able to choose the events that roll through our lives but we have enormous power over how those events affect our lives.

☞   Uncover the Hidden Beliefs

As I moved through the blast zone and the long process of putting things back together again, I questioned over and over and over what I truly believed about my life and my self. It was unsettling to realize many of the stories I'd told myself weren't helpful and weren't even necessarily, or at least not exclusively, true.

Our beliefs about ourselves are often like Russian nesting dolls' each one a shell that, once cracked, lets us see another, deeper, hidden treasure. These beliefs, true or otherwise, are crucial aspects of the ego identity we create, the fence and face we build to move through this world. They are critically important in shaping how we experience life, so examining and questioning them can have profound results.

On a sheet of paper, write down the beliefs about yourself that you think of as positive. My original list looked something like this:

☞   Strong
☞   Tough

☞ Hard worker

☞ Smart

☞ Altruistic

☞ Great dog owner

Now, take a moment to consider each one and why you believe it, why you have identified with it. See if there is a deeper belief underneath that might not be so positive. For example, I believed myself to be strong and tough, a fighter. I valued being so tough because that was what my father, who had some pretty messed-up beliefs of his own, praised me for. I identified as a hard worker because I'd been told, and believed, that life was hard, but by God I wasn't going to let it beat me. And guess what? Up to that point I'd created a life in which I had to be tough and I had to fight! I could with all honesty also have added open, receptive, easily attracts support, and efficient, but I didn't because at the time those were not the traits I valued about myself.

Often in doing core-belief work we are instructed to examine the negative beliefs and question whether or not they are really true. This is useful work. I do it myself and I encourage it for everyone working to improve their lives and our world. However, in my experience the gold is in finding the deeper, subconscious limiting beliefs that parade as positive. Looking at the hidden plots behind the beliefs we *want* to hold about ourselves is a powerful way to go about this. Ask yourself why it was important for you to put those particular traits and characteristics in the positive column. But don't get too carried away or overly critical—I mean, come on, being a great dog owner is one hundred percent a fully positive trait!

☞ Add Some Feeling to Your Meditation

One form of meditation is to practice *feeling* a certain way. According to neuroscience, our brains do not distinguish between actually doing something and genuinely imagining doing it. This is why top-level athletes spend time envisioning themselves sailing over the high-jump bar, hitting a home run, sticking a perfect landing, or draining a perfect three-point game-winning basket. In *Spiritual Economics*, Eric Butterworth refers to this embodied meditation and visualization as "Imagineering." That is a fantastic term because genuinely imagining doing something creates new neural pathways in the brain. Maybe that's what Einstein was getting at when he said, "Imagination is more important than knowledge."

We are usually taught that feelings happen to us, that they are something we have to deal with and are beyond our control. We believe the things that happen to us cause us to feel a certain way and sometimes, especially in really intense experiences, that's true. However, we also have the ability to choose how we feel and doing so directly influences our experience of things that are happening to and around us. Our minds generate thoughts. Thoughts generate feelings.

This is not about faking it till you make it; it's not about superficial appearances but is, rather, about actually conjuring up a feeling. Gratitude is a great place to start. Imagine a time in your life when you were genuinely grateful for something or somebody. Notice how it feels in your body. Where is the sensation? For example, my gratitude sensation is usually right in the middle of my chest and upper rib cage. Put your hand on that place on your body that has a physical sensation related to the feeling of gratitude. Saying "thank you" produces more things to *be* thankful for. This isn't just playing Pollyanna but is, in fact, one of the most powerful ways to bring some relief when feeling crushed by heavy and hard events and circumstances. Feeling grateful for anything, big or small, shifts your mind off the problem, at least for a moment.

You can do this same feeling exercise with feelings of love, accomplishment, joy, etc. This practice is incredibly effective in adjusting the lens we put on our lives because thoughts and feelings are a two-way street. Thoughts generate feelings *and* feelings can cause us to think certain types of thoughts. When we are dealing with the hard stuff life throws at us, it is so easy to be consumed by fear, anger, hurt, blame, hatred, powerlessness. When your mind is trapped on a hamster wheel of negative and painful thoughts, unable to stop the spinning, one way to slow the wheel is to embody, to imagine the sensation of positive emotions. It throws an interrupt into the cycle and gives you the power to choose again.

Volumes of scientific research into how the brain works have given us insight into the direct connection between our thoughts, our feelings and our body chemistry. As soon as a person has a thought, a certain type of chemical is released into the body. Positive thoughts release pleasant-feeling chemicals; negative thoughts release stress-related chemicals. As we think certain types of thoughts over and over again, we are literally training our physical bodies to feel a certain way. Over time this forms emotional habits and our general state of being is under the control of conditioned responses driven by chemistry, created by thoughts we usually don't even know we are having.

The great news is that we can change our habitual state of being by training ourselves to notice our thoughts and replace negative thoughts with positive ones. This is where the "Choose Again" exercise I mentioned above proves extremely useful. Notice the thought, shift it to something, and then imagine feeling different, better, right then and there. It takes vigilance and practice but over time you can literally train yourself to be naturally happier, more peaceful, and more successful.

There are a million ways to view every challenging situation we deal with. Stuff happens. Life is messy and unpredictable and sometimes downright brutal. The power is in pausing just a moment before slapping a snap judgment on what's taking place. As soon as you decide what it is, or that it's bad, why not pause just for a second and ask, "Maybe there's a different way to look at this? What have I got to lose by asking?" After all, we can always go back to viewing it the way we were before. This is not about playing ostrich, sticking your head in the sand and ignoring things that need to be dealt with, and it's not just blind faith. It's about opening up to the truth that there is always more to every situation—more potential, more possibilities, more solutions—than a first-blush judgment might reveal.

CHAPTER 9

Reentering the Arena

"It takes a special valor to have your heart broken, your pride hammered, your failure and humiliation made public, to be driven out and ridiculed and then choose to pick up, dust off, and go back in."

—*Cylvia Hayes*

ome experiences just change us. Period. Life casts us from the path we thought we'd walk and we simply are not who or how we were before. Just like rebuilding a city after a major earthquake, hurricane, or wildfire, creating the new you takes some time and usually happens in phases.

Reengaging with friends, family, and community after a life-changing trauma, especially one that other people know about, can be a trying process. Like relearning to walk after a severely broken leg, reengaging with others after catastrophic life change can be unsteady and it may hurt in places it didn't use to. Some of this is about how people react to us and some is about our own changed reactions.

In her work as a shame researcher, Brené Brown makes beautiful use of the metaphor of entering the arena, stepping out into life, and taking risks. We all face many arenas—taking a new job, dealing with a difficult boss in an old job, starting a business, going to school, opening our hearts to love, or the terrifying arena of putting ourselves out there for public office or trying to share our talents with the world, hoping it likes what we're offering.

Doing any of those things takes courage, but that effort pales in comparison to the courage it takes to reenter after you've had your ass kicked in the arena. Making a costly mistake, losing a loved one, suffering an assault, witnessing something terrible, or experiencing humiliation or ostracism can make us want to contract, pull in, and try to protect ourselves. That's a natural and understandable reaction but too much of it can cost a life worth living.

Of all the losses I experienced during the public shaming, one of the most unexpected and disturbing was the loss of a natural sense of safety and trust. I had believed most people were basically good people and that no one really just wanted to hurt me. Yet there I was under continuous, seemingly widespread, often vicious and personal verbal and written attack. My psyche was shocked by the amount of hatred and ugliness raining down on me. I couldn't believe so many total strangers would so want to do me harm. I clearly had had no idea how much jealousy and animosity fellow colleagues and political players had held.

Once again, my naiveté rocked me. Had I just been living in some alternate reality, completely clueless about myself and everyone else?

The jumbled feelings of abandonment, fear, anger, uncertainty, and humiliation, combined with the need to be constantly on the lookout for reporters, began to change me. I became afraid to go out into public, worried that the vileness of the online trollosphere and anonymous hate-mailers and callers would meet me face-to-face. Before I'd leave my house I'd sneak to a window to see if the coast was clear and triple-check that every door and window was locked—something I hadn't done in the once seemingly safe little neighborhood. While jogging, if I saw someone approaching I would get suspicious and guarded and if possible, move to the other side of the street or take a side trail.

My trauma had been so public and widespread that at first even the grocery store seemed like a dangerous coliseum. My face was plastered all over the newspapers near the checkout stands and I felt grossly exposed and vulnerable. I was barely inside Safeway's automatic doors when a man recognized me. I slammed my guard up as he approached, steeled for insult. Instead he said gently, "I'm so sorry about what they're doing to you guys. I hope you're okay. I've always appreciated your work." I let out a choked breath, said something I don't remember, thanked him for his kind words, and quickly turned away blinking back tears.

I can't even count how many times a variation of that type of encounter took place. The more I steeled myself, the more I began to harden, to close down and wall myself away from others. And yet, even as that was happening, I continued doing the inner work, the therapy and meditation, and working with *A Course in Miracles*. Over time I realized that if I allowed the trauma to change my basic personality—the warm, open, mostly trusting person that was my true nature—then the attackers had indeed won. If I closed down opportunities for beautiful chance encounters and unexpected new friends due to fear of hurled insults, I would truly be the loser. And so, I made a conscious decision to stay open and trust in goodness.

One of my bolder reentry moves was attending a journalism conference in Portland which a number of my media assailants were attending. I couldn't pass up a conference on ethics in journalism when I had experienced such blatantly unethical behavior from the state's largest newspapers. I also couldn't pass up the opportunity to stand up to my attackers and show that I wasn't just going to go crawl into a ditch somewhere.

The drive toward the conference center felt like approaching a lion's den. Amazingly, I flipped on the radio to find Jon Ronson, author of *So, You've Been Publicly Shamed?*, being interviewed. I took it as a sign from Source and, as they say, screwed my courage to the sticking place.

Walking up to the building my hands were shaking and my breathing shallow. I took a seat in the back of the auditorium feeling vulnerable and unsafe, like an animal of prey. Holding myself like iron, I pretended not to notice all the surreptitious stares and whispers.

Shortly after I sat down, a young woman approached and asked if I was Cylvia Hayes. I said, "Yes, who are you?" She was an intern with the *Willamette Week*. Instantly, I felt as though I was holding a poisonous snake with my bare hand. She asked if she could take my picture. I said emphatically, "No," then turned my back to her. She stammered a bit, then left.

I left at lunch break because I thought they'd probably pounce. They did. I sat alone in my car, eating a sandwich and listening to the *Talk Out Loud* radio show live-streaming from the conference. The so-called journalists hammered on about the unproved allegations and mockingly asked if I wanted to come up on stage for an interview. *Yeah, right.* I had so far managed to avoid the deer-in-the-headlights moment and hoped to keep it that way.

Later that afternoon, two reporters with *Journalism that Matters* and *American Public Media* introduced themselves, saying they knew of my situation and the witch hunt that was taking place. Linda Miller spent a long time with me that day sharing her story of leaving mainstream "gotcha" media for the emerging fields of "solutions journalism" and "restoration narratives." This information would prove to be important to my own professional reemergence many months from then. Knowing there were factions of the press trying to address the damage done by the scandal-driven click-for-cash model was hopeful. More immediately, Miller's basic, genuine kindness in the tension of the lion's den warmed and grounded me. To this day I am very grateful she took that time with me.

The most absurd moments came during the lunch panel that included the sitting news editor of *Willamette Week*. I sat there digesting my sandwich, trying hard not to choke as I listened to him, on stage, pontificating about how hard

Willamette Week worked to tell the truth. Saying that, "Right next to truth is the commitment to transparency." Several people in the room looked over at me as he was speaking. It was all I could do not to spout, "That is such a crock of shit!" Linda Miller had sat just behind me and she reached up and tapped my shoulder. I looked back and she rolled her eyes.

As the session ended and people began filing out of the room, the news editor approached and said, "Hello, Cylvia. It's nice to finally meet you in person."

I stayed calm and tried not to just see him as an object of my hatred. I said, "Nice to meet you." He asked why I was there. "As I said yesterday, I am just here to listen and learn." He asked what I had taken away so far. I said, "There is a lot of interesting discussion of ethics, and lack thereof, in media and journalism. That's a topic I'm very interested in just now." His face flickered a bit. I picked up my coffee and left.

I really don't remember much of the content from that conference, but that wasn't the point. I do remember that when I arrived on day two, my hands weren't shaking. I sat in the back of the auditorium, focused on breathing deeply. Reminding myself that I wasn't going to harden, I worked on intentionally seeing the people in the room not as dangerous enemies but as fellow human beings. I chose again and again and again not to focus on the hatred that wanted to surface. The experience was terribly stressful, but I was glad I did it. I was proud of my courage and my ability to hold my head up and claim my right to be there.

When we go through those truly life-altering events, we will never be the same again. We won't have a choice to go back. The choice will be whether we become harder and more closed-off or softer and more expansive. We can refuse to trust anyone, including God or Life itself, and plaster some more bricks into our fortress. Or, we can harness the pain and allow the tears to wash away the walls, giving our hearts more space to stretch, expand, and love.

I didn't make a habit of attending journalism conferences or putting myself in the path of my attackers, but I did face a million mini-reentries. One day I was at the gym and the publisher of my hometown paper, the *Bend Bulletin*, came in. Weeks earlier he had written an editorial filled with speculation put forward as fact; in it he had called me a "con artist."

Spikes of adrenaline shot through my body but I was determined not to run away. I steeled myself, walked up to him, and said, "I am not a con artist." A small, elderly white man, he looked up at me, flushed bright red, and quickly looked away. I said, "That was a cheap shot. The picture you have painted of me is not true." He muttered something and turned to move away from me so fast he nearly ran into the wall.

It's one thing to rip into somebody sitting behind the shield of your computer screen or institution. It's something else again to do it face-to-face.

While there were a few of these intense encounters, perhaps the most amazing thing was that I was never attacked face-to-face. In fact, people—from neighbors to complete strangers—went out of their way to be kind and each time I was greeted with kindness, a little healing took place.

There was also an odd sort of liberation that came with the public scrutiny of my emails and personal records. Yes, my personal communications had been spread around, which was a tremendous violation. The darkest, ugliest, most humiliating aspects of my past had been laid out for the world to see and hear and judge. And yet, I still stood. I still grew. The mob, wanting to tear off my limbs, had ripped through three hundred and thirty thousand pages of my work, my thoughts, and my interactions and had found nothing they could stick their pitchforks into. I doubted many of the people who were conjuring the attacks or piling on could have stood as strong in a similar position. It reminded me of one of my favorite quotes from Theodore Roosevelt's *Man in the Arena*.

> *It is not the critic who counts: not the man who points out how the strong man stumbles or where the doer of deeds could have done better. The credit belongs to the man who is actually in the arena, whose face is marred by dust and sweat and blood, who strives valiantly, who errs and comes up short again and again, because there is no effort without error or shortcoming, but who knows the great enthusiasms, the great devotions, who spends himself for a worthy cause; who, at the best, knows, in the end, the triumph of high achievement, and who, at the worst, if he fails, at least he fails while daring greatly, so that his place shall never be with those cold and timid souls who knew neither victory nor defeat.*

I began to sense that at some point this experience and exposure would empower me, free my voice, and make me more fearless in my life and in the work I had dedicated that life to.

Over time, as I healed, I became frustrated that the shaming was always the first thing anyone would ask about, especially if they hadn't seen me since before it had set in. I understood. Most people were curious to know how I and John were holding up after something so horrific, and many were genuinely concerned. But I was getting frustrated with it, ready to move on, or so I thought.

People continued to ask and I continued to be frustrated until something really uncomfortable happened a few times. I'd be in a conversation and we'd be talking about the big ordeal and the person would say, "Wow, I had no idea," or "I really haven't heard anything about what you've been through, but …" Once, I was giving a little speech to a small women's group and as I launched into the story, I saw one woman do an eye roll. And that's when I realized, *Oh, my God, it's not just them leading with it. It's me!*

Ugghh. I had allowed myself to become so identified with the trauma, with the "big ordeal" that I just assumed each person I met knew about it and was going to ask about it. That was a mistake. A whole lot of people didn't know, and most didn't really care.

I realized I needed a new story and a reentry plan. I made it a point to stop assuming people were going to ask about the trauma and I designed ways to redirect the conversation if they did. I didn't do this because I was ashamed of what had happened; I did it because I didn't want to continue identifying with the trauma. I didn't want to stay stuck in an unhealthy relationship with the terrible, tragic story. It wasn't about being dishonest, just intentional.

Whenever we are going through something truly traumatic, especially if other people know about it, it pays to be prepared ahead of time for our reentry into community and society. The loss of a loved one, the terrible decision that seriously harmed someone, being attacked, the prison sentence, the incurable diagnosis; these things change us and they change how people react to us. Being prepared and intentional gives us more control over the conditions of our reentry.

People's reactions to our changes are one thing, and ours are another. On the heels of heavy life challenges, certain places, activities, people, and even topics of conversation can leave us feeling more vulnerable, focusing on the loss or rehashing the ugly memories. Becoming more conscious of our reactions to certain people, settings, or activities gives us an opportunity to decide whether or not we want to continue to play in those arenas. Sometimes, the answer is yes, but in order to be at ease we need to approach the activity or engagement differently, with a different attitude or set of expectations. Other times, we may come to see that certain arenas that used to draw us in are really just coliseums, battlefields that never were good for us, and we can choose not to reenter at all.

Another aspect of this is that our own internal desires and priorities may shift. One of the reasons releasing our attachment to ego is so challenging is that we worry it will require us to change. Be warned. It will! When we open up to the deeper mysteries of our broken moments we often experience profound shifts in our preferences and goals. This can run the gamut from becoming intolerant of certain TV shows and songs to being pulled toward an entire career change.

During my long multiyear stretch of reinventing my career, community, and self, while feeling held down and held back due to the ongoing legal and media challenges, I often struggled with feeling that I wasn't making a big enough contribution. Before my life blew up I had felt like I was being well used working on the big issues I cared so much about. For three and a half years I sat in a liminal phase, unsure of my position in society and not knowing if I would ever again be able to contribute much to the causes to which I'd dedicated my life.

As things settled down and I was able to restart some aspects of my consulting business I landed a few clients, but my heart wasn't in it. Over time I had to admit I no longer had any passion for the type of work I'd been so committed to before. Having seen how deeply flawed our political and governance systems are, I had no passion left for it.

This was a bit of a disturbing existential crisis because I had put so many years and so much effort into that line of work and had based a lot of my sense of importance on that work. It was unsettling to think about letting it go because it felt like losing another part of my previous life, like the opponent had indeed beaten me. But I knew it was right. I had changed too much to go back to what I was doing before. Something in me sensed it would be wasting the new depths I'd been plumbing to go back to the same work.

In an odd paradox, on one hand I sensed that the inner work was a worthy cause in its own right; on the other I harbored a fear that so strongly prioritizing the inner journey would lead to retreating from my lifelong desire to make a positive difference in our world. I didn't know what to make of it, but I couldn't retreat form the inner work; I was compelled.

Over time, as I moved forward clearing away the rubble from the blown-up life I had known, I came to see that I wasn't losing the desire to make a difference, I was just being directed to go about it very, very differently.

My true north hadn't changed but my True Self was emerging. I still wanted to make a big positive difference with my life. I still wanted to do what I could to help heal our planet and give people in difficult circumstances a way to rise up. But I knew the way I would work toward that goal was forever changed and so I let go for a time, gave space to the uncertainty, and let the shift happen.

The reentry process went to a whole new level in March 2018 when I was scheduled to speak at the big TEDx event in my hometown of Bend, Oregon. This would be the first time I had spoken publicly about the experience of having my familiar identity attacked and cracked and the process of opening and deepening that was resulting. News that I was going to be a speaker caused quite a buzz and not everybody liked it. One major sponsor pulled its support from the event and that was hurtful because the business in question had a lot of ties to people who had previously supported me but apparently had bought into the smear campaign. There was absolutely nothing I could do about it. I received anonymous threats of violence if I didn't back out of the event and the event organizers received warnings that hecklers would be on site and decided to hire additional security.

Just days before the event, the *Oregonian* let it be known that, several months earlier, they had placed a lien on my house to try to force me to pay the attorney's fees they'd racked up going through my emails. I hadn't been informed they had filed a lien and suspected they had timed the news to drop right before my TEDx talk.

Despite it all I stayed the course and so did the event organizers. I was beyond impressed that the TEDx Bend organizing committee, true to TED form, did not back down but stood behind me as the event approached.

It took me a lot longer than I expected to finalize my talk; I just couldn't get it to a place that felt right. The pieces finally clicked into place when I stopped thinking about what I wanted to get out of the talk and instead became very still and quiet and asked what could the talk do for those who would hear it. In other words, what were the key pieces from my experience of public trauma and ego revelation that could be helpful to people in the audience. With about a week left before the event I knew exactly what I wanted to offer. I practiced my talk and worked through scenarios for how I would handle potential hecklers.

I was surprisingly calm stepping onto the stage as it dawned on me that I could stand there with gibberish falling from my mouth and people laughing or I could get pelted with tomatoes and none of it would be as bad as what I had already been through. Like I'd suspected, being publicly shamed is indeed very liberating!

As I'd feared I got emotional when I mentioned the damage I'd caused to John. The audience was silent, rapt as I worked to get my voice back under control. Once I did, I noted that despite the hardship, John and I were still together and when I pointed out that he was in the audience right there, the place erupted in applause. Throughout my entire talk I felt nothing but warmth and support, and at the end they lifted me up with a standing ovation. Having had to stay silent for so long due to all the legal proceedings, it felt incredibly good to finally have a chance to give voice to my experience of events that had been so skewed by the media. Being able to stand publicly and take responsibility for my mistake and share some of what I had been learning was a tremendously healing experience and I was touched and very grateful that, having been steeled for ugliness, I received only love and support. I stepped off the stage and returned a little more confidently to my life.

It takes a special valor to have our heart broken, our pride hammered, our failures or humiliation made public, to be driven out and ridiculed and then choose to pick up, dust off, and go back in. Reentering certain arenas will be the hardest thing we ever do, but it's how we grow, reclaim our power, and build a life that makes a difference. *How* we reenter can make a big difference. There will be changes in the landscape of our life and relationships and there is much we can do to shape those changes so that they move us in positive, productive directions. Allowing space for change and growth is how we reclaim our power and place. Sometimes our mess becomes our most important message and our personal examples of harnessing adversity to grow and deepen shine powerful lights for others who are navigating dark times.

Strategies for Empowered Reentry

☞ Develop answers to key questions ahead of time

There are a few key questions to consider in figuring out your strategy for reengaging with friends, social circles, and community post-trauma.

☞ How will you answer when they ask, "How are you?"
☞ How will you answer if they ask about the traumatic event?
☞ How do you want to show up energetically?

The answers to these questions are personal and individualized. You will find your own answers as you move forward reclaiming your place in the reshaped world. The most important thing is not to assume each person you meet is going to lead with the trauma and to have a concise, empowered-feeling answer if they do.

For me, when someone would bring up the shaming and ongoing media assaults, I learned to say something along the lines of, "Well, it has certainly been intense and really challenging, but it's also produced the most profound growth of my entire life and that's what I'm focusing on." I always made a point of thanking people for their genuine kindness and concern. It was important to me to show up with kindness, strength, and as an example that even something as horrific as what I'd experienced could produce growth and peace.

As I began to rebuild my career and open up for new clients and potential job positions, I made another intentional adjustment to my story. I was a fifty-year-old woman rebuilding from the destruction of what had already been an unconventional career path. I had a three-year gap in any substantive professional work positions. I could have led with the story of, "Well, I made a huge mistake and was publicly shamed and derailed," but instead, I explained, "My life partner and I had a very difficult thing happen and I decided to deal with it by taking a sabbatical to do some deep inner work, write a book, get a coaching certification, and complete the first stage of a master's in divinity program." Both responses were true.

Without shirking any responsibility, there are a dozen ways to describe the things we've done and the things done to us. We can't change what happened but we *can* change the story we tell about it, after all, our stories are ours to write and rewrite as necessary. We might as well take control of our own narrative and tell an empowered tale. Being intentional with our story helps smooth the bumps so we can reenter the arena on our own terms.

☞ Have a few trusted sticky people you can be really real with

I've always been someone that, when asked how I was doing, would tell the truth even if it wasn't pretty. That changed during my long ordeal. It wasn't about being dishonest but about not wanting to focus on and rehash the hurt. And yet, we're human beings, and the deep hurts can't always stay buried, at least not without oozing out in some other unhealthy eruption. It is crucial to have someone you can really share with. For me, that had always been John, but in the first two years of our trauma he was often hurting so much himself, I didn't want to add to his angst. Thank God a couple of friends stepped up to provide that much needed supportive outlet. Over time my mom also became a trusted friend and counsel.

We were four years into our ordeal when John finally opened up to me about some of his deepest feelings about the role I had played in the mess that exploded our lives. He had harbored a lot more resentment than he'd let on. It was hard for me to hear, but I knew he needed to express it. And the truth was, I'd already been feeling it for years! It was a subtle distancing he had adopted, a little shield that had been put up between us. He had kept most of his deepest hurts and anger toward me and many, many others to himself and it had altered his personality in ways that had been hard for me to witness and experience. He had lost his joy and sparkle and seemed to just be dragging through life. Finally, his expression of those deeper wounds and vulnerability and my newfound, hard-earned maturity and lack of reactivity cracked open a dam that let old backed-up, stagnant waters wash away.

Almost instantly, John's demeanor shifted; he seemed lighter and straighter and more joyful. Part of me wished he'd opened up to me about it years earlier, but I knew he had his own journey and in truth, years earlier I wouldn't have been secure enough, or loving enough, to hear him out, feel the sting, and not open my mouth in rebuttal. Over the next few weeks we did discuss these issues again and there was no charge, just beautiful, mutually supportive listening.

☞   Celebrate the full-spiral moments

As our healing progressed, John and I both experienced moments where we'd go somewhere we hadn't been since much earlier in our ordeal and we'd be swept with a realization of how very different life was for us compared to the previous time we'd visited that place. Usually this was a super-positive feeling. I can't recall how many times I've said to myself or to John, "Man, my life is in such a better place than it was when I was last here." Other times the feeling was a little sad, a remembrance of loss or hurt, and sometimes it was just noticing that I no longer cared for a place that used to mean something to me.

I like the term *full spiral*, rather than full circle, because we don't ever come back to exactly the same place we were before. Even when we're repeating experiences or patterns of behavior, we are not in exactly the same place. As the Greek philosopher Heraclitus said, "No man ever steps in the same river twice, for it's not the same river and he's not the same man."

As spiritual beings we are always evolving and shifting even while doing things we have done many times before. It may feel as though we are circling back around to something familiar but we are at a different level of consciousness and experience. This is especially true when coming out after a catastrophic life event and those full-spiral moments, when reentering an old arena after a major loss, change, and transition, are powerful opportunities to get a sense of just how much you've changed and grown. Sometimes you lay new memories down over certain places and events. Sometimes you realize old familiar places or people no longer hold your interest. Sometimes you look upon one who has been through the fire with you and see them as older, more scarred, and immeasurably more beautiful.

Reentering the arena isn't for wimps. Reclaiming our place after a catastrophe takes massive courage. In cultural rites-of-passage rituals, initiates are stripped of their old place in society and, after a period of time, are granted a new role and a new place in the community. When coming through intense life trauma, and our own personal, individual liminal experiences, the point is not to wait for someone else to bestow our new position upon us, but to remember who we are, that we are worthy, and that we have something of value to offer, and then intentionally claim our place once again.

When we've made it that far, we've survived something that likely would have destroyed many. That's the time to feel our strength, make the choice to push through, to love, to strive, to put ourselves fully out there once again. You have the right to reenter any arena you choose, and the right and the power to be wherever you choose to be. Our world is made better through witnessing our courage.

This poem brought me comfort during some tough stretches of my journey. May it do the same for you, a fellow magnificent, uniquely beautiful, and unconquerable soul.

Invictus

Out of the night that covers me,
Black as the pit from pole to pole,

I thank whatever gods may be
For my unconquerable soul.

In the fell clutch of circumstance
I have not winced nor cried aloud.
Under the bludgeonings of chance
My head is bloody, but unbowed.

Beyond this place of wrath and tears
Looms but the Horror of the shade,
And yet the menace of the years
Finds and shall find me unafraid.

It matters not how strait the gate,
How charged with punishments the scroll,
I am the master of my fate,
I am the captain of my soul.
—William Ernest Henley

One day as I was navigating my reentry into society, I was out hiking and came across a crow trying to eat a snail. The fierce black beauty pecked and poked the glossy spiral shell, tossing it this way and that, but the snail stayed tucked up tight. After much pecking and head cocking, the crow gave up and took flight. Several moments later, the brave little snail tentatively unfurled its delicate antennae and long, soft body and slid forward in search of food and other snail interests.

We are like that too. Each of us on these spiraling human journeys faces this same choice over and over again. Do we play it safe and keep our shields up, protected from potential pain or attack? Or do we stretch out our soft inner selves and move forward exposing our vulnerable places in order to find sustenance, love, and life itself? Clearing away the rubble of withdrawal, guardedness, and fear is a critical step in moving beyond surviving to full-on thriving, moving from cautious reentry to glorious resurrection.

Part Three:

*Resurrection
Re-Membering
Rebuilding Self with
a Capital "S"*

CHAPTER 10

The Great Unlearning

"The most important part of learning is to unlearn our errors."

—*Greek philosopher Zeno*

My intention with this book was to share elements of my traumatic experience in a way that could be useful to anyone going through times of major life upheaval and transition. Surviving and reinventing from my long ordeal led me to discover and invent some practical tools and strategies that improved every aspect of my life and are helping the people I support through my reinvention and empowerment coaching practice. I have shared the most valuable of those strategies and practices in the earlier chapters of this book. I wanted to deliver concrete, doable solutions to readers and I hope I hit that mark.

However, practical, powerful survival tools were just the tip of the iceberg of what my dark night experience delivered. Not only did I learn to do things differently but also to see differently, believe differently, and *be* differently.

The final section of this book describes, as best I can, the mind-blowing, life-changing transformation of perception, perspective, and possibilities that resulted from having my old, familiar persona blown apart. I share it as encouragement and food for thought for anyone moving through times of major transition and reinvention.

Even just a few months into my ordeal, when the circumstances ripping through my life were still extremely difficult, I was already excited about the personal and spiritual learning I was experiencing. A few years later, once the traumatic events finally reached conclusion, the dust settled, and the reshaped landscape of my new life emerged, I came to see that the real treasure was in the *unlearning*.

As I was well into writing this book, and after years of working with the spiritual teachers and therapeutic strategies described herein, I had a profound realization. It wasn't agenda-driven media or political attackers who blew my life up; it was me. More specifically, it was the catastrophic, destructive power of my unexamined ego.

The First Lady position had been extremely difficult from the beginning; I should have seen it coming but at the time wasn't self-aware enough to do so. There were many aspects that made the situation so challenging.

First, Oregon had never had a highly engaged, business-owning, policy-oriented First Lady before and the bulk of the institution did not welcome the change. John and I had envisioned working together on the issues we both cared so much about but we had been naïve about the amount of resistance there would be to having a First Lady openly engaged in the substantive work of the administration. There just was no handbook, or even established precedent, for the position.

Second was the deeply imbedded institutional sexism and misogynistic media climate. At that point in my life I had been a heavy equipment operator, had played men's soccer and ridden rodeo, but I had never faced the level of gender-role prejudice the way I did in the political arena, particularly in the bizarre position of "First Lady" to a powerful man.

And then there was the situation with the bizarre title of "First Lady." I hadn't intended to take the title because we weren't married and I wasn't attached to a title, but people immediately began using it. Either they thought we were married, or they didn't care. At first when I was referred to as First Lady, I would try to explain, "Well, not really since we're not married. I'm just first partner trying to do some good work," etc., etc. It was especially awkward because there was a vocal minority of people who hated the fact that John and I were together but unmarried and who routinely beat me up in the papers and cyberspace because of it.

One unexpected series of events sort of sums up my first couple of years in the awkward position. In winter 2012, western Oregon was experiencing monsoonal rain and the Humane Society near the capital flooded, forcing them to evacuate the animals. Mary, my assistant, who was also an animal lover and one of Tessa's many occasional caretakers, alerted me to the situation at the Humane Society. She and I thought we could use the large basement in Mahonia Hall to house critters for a couple of days until they could be returned to the shelter.

I wound up with two small crates, each containing a cat from the sick ward that I hadn't even seen, and a small silver pit bull, appropriately named Blue, that no one else had wanted to take. Back at Mahonia Hall, I put each of the crated cats into upstairs bedrooms and then introduced Blue to Tessa. She seemed friendly enough, so I decided to let her hang out with us rather than locking her in the basement.

Good gracious! She was a hyperactive menace that first night, ripping and snorting around the big house, chasing Tessa. But after a couple of days away from the shelter she calmed and became a funny, loving little dog. I realized had she been any other breed, she would have had a home, so I decided to play my First Lady card to try to get her one.

I ran Facebook posts about Blue. The *Oregonian* wrote a story about it that included a line about the pit bull "shacking up" at Mahonia Hall. The online commenters and cyber-trolls went wild with a barrage of nasty comments about the slutty, unmarried "shack-up honey" to the governor.

That evening the woman from the Humane Society returned Blue after a failed adoption appointment at the shelter. She said, "Wow, I've waited my whole life to meet someone more controversial than a pit bull!" Apparently, she had read the story and reader comments. It was funny, and also deeply frustrating.

Snarky comments aside, we did find grinning Blue a permanent home. Six other pit bulls were also adopted or fostered away from the shelter and the two scraggly cats settled into their new posh lives at the governor's mansion far more easily than I was settling into being First Lady.

The cats were happy, but I was as depressed as I'd ever been and I realize now it was due to my damned ego, to my concocted subconscious belief that I was small, alone, weak, and not really worth very much. That false identity, sense of aloneness, and need to fight to protect myself was the bomb that blew up my life and ricocheted shrapnel into the lives of those I loved.

Part of the problem lay in why I took on the First Lady role in the first place. The healthy aspect of motivation was that I wanted to be part of big, positive change and I believed John was the right person at the right time for the governor's position. He proved this true through the transformative work he delivered. The less healthy motivation was that as much as I wanted to make a big contribution on issues I cared about, although I never would have admitted it at the time, I didn't really believe I was capable of doing it on my own. My inner sense of littleness couldn't see the value in the work I was delivering in my own right and so I leaped at the new opportunity and put all of the good work in jeopardy.

Once in the First Lady position, I worked my tail off on issues I cared about—climate change, environmental protection, poverty and economic justice, and to this day I am grateful for and proud of that work. However, the good work wasn't enough; I still felt unsupported, like I had to fight for myself. I still feared I'd wind up on the other side of the position with nothing to really show for it, having to claw my way back into my business and career. I wanted to do the good work, but by God, I wanted to get the credit for it too.

It was a genuinely challenging and awkward position. However, with distance and more wisdom, I now see that even before everything blew to pieces, I had made it far more difficult for myself and for John than it needed to be. Had I truly believed in myself and the value of my service, and had I known that I am not just a small, unsafe, in-it-by-myself, isolated being, I would have handled it much differently. I literally created a battlefield that didn't need to exist and marched into a war of my own creation. Not only did I make things unnecessarily miserable for me and John, but by pushing so hard and making sure that my name was on all my work, I gave the political and media attackers so much more fodder than they would have had otherwise.

The unique challenges of the First Lady position and my unrealistic expectations around it created the perfect storm to blow my unexamined ego right out into the spotlight, figuratively and literally.

I had to acknowledge that I'd created a potent personality, a huge fortress of individuality that was a powerful tool for keeping the terrible unrecognized sense of inadequacy and aloneness at bay. I was the fricking Darth Vader of egos! I was super powerful, a force, but I hadn't done enough of the deep work to keep that power from turning destructive. The irony is the ego persona I'd created as an unconscious attempt at self-protection had in fact robbed me of peace and genuine power and created a huge and costly mess.

True dark night of the soul experiences rock us to the core and shake the very foundations of our belief systems and indeed, I found myself questioning everything so much and so hard that I even began to question my own sanity, or whether I'd ever even had any. *Was anything I'd believed about myself true? Did I know myself at all? Was there any God or higher power involved in any of this or was life just a random clusterfuck? Who was I?* What *was I? Was everything I believed about myself, other people, my work, politics, the world, God, and reality just a bunch of misguided crap?* The terrifying and liberating answer to that question was mostly yes!

Prior to my big shake-up I had believed what I believed based on what I thought to be rational decisions and direct experiences. In fact, if you had asked me then what I believed, I would have very clearly and solidly articulated my take on how the world worked, what I stood for, what kind of person I was, and even what I believed God to be. Most of what I told you wouldn't have been true. It's not that I would have intentionally lied; it's just that I really didn't have a clue.

I would have said that I believed I was basically a good person who had committed my life to trying to protect the environment and help humanity shift to a saner economic system. If pressed I would have had the courage to admit that some part of me tended to believe I wasn't good enough and was inadequate, but that I had done a lot of work in dealing with that issue.

What I wouldn't have said, couldn't have said, because I didn't yet know, was that much of my seeming altruism was also serving a deep desire to feel important and valuable. I wouldn't, couldn't, have told you that my deepest terrible belief wasn't that I wasn't good enough, but that I was fundamentally unsafe and utterly alone and that I'd better fight like hell to protect myself because nobody else was going to do it for me. I also couldn't have told you that I was far more than just a good person because I hadn't met that me yet.

The pre-blast Cylvia would have told you I believed we were all spiritual beings and that our souls were more than just these human lives. And I would have said I believed, somehow, all of life was connected. But underneath that layer, in a place I hadn't yet looked, was a deep and terrible belief in separateness and aloneness that still held remnants of belief in a God "out there" that could be a tough, judgmental, terrifying tyrant.

Back then had you asked me, I could have spouted plenty of conventional wisdom I believed in because I hadn't yet grown enough to see, that for the most part, conventional wisdom is an oxymoron. Most of what this world tells us is real and wise is actually just the product of one illusion piled upon another and one ego trying to get something from another ego in a desperate attempt to address the terrible sense of separation and powerlessness. Back then, without realizing it, I was still under the confines of a lifetime of programming and unquestioned false beliefs.

Most of us receive some form of that limiting and unhealthy type of programming from the time we are little children. In addition to what we get from our parents and caretakers, our current consumption-crazed, celebrity worshipping, clickbait-driven culture is a thick marinade of not-enoughness, isolation, and separation. This instills in us the deeply disempowering habit of comparing ourselves to others and finding ourselves and our lives lacking so that we will buy, buy, buy things to make it better, serving the zealous God of consumerism in hope of salvation.

Comparison is the death of creativity and peace and yet most of us are totally addicted and conditioned to it. And here's the doubly crazy thing—most of the time in this edited, Photoshopped, airbrushed world we're not even comparing ourselves to real people. We're measuring ourselves against illusions! What could be more damaging to our sense of worth? Each one of us is a totally unique creation with a completely diverse background and experience. We are literally incomparable.

In addition to and related to family and cultural programming, many of us are also hit with religious traditions that drive a sense of separation and unworthiness deep into our psyches. Looking back at my own life experience I now see that the most damaging and limiting abuse I experienced as a child was the religious abuse that instilled the terrible and terrifying notion of a separate, unknowable, and untrustworthy God. I do not blame those who taught me such terrible concepts. They did so out of love and fear, in an effort to protect me from the beliefs they themselves held as a result of powerful programming they'd been fed.

As my spiritual quickening moved along and my questioning deepened, I gained access to ways of shifting old beliefs and assumptions that were keeping me trapped in littleness and fear. The more deeply I questioned, the more clearly I came to see that I had been playing on a two-dimensional game board, unaware of the true power of our minds, perception, and programming. Over time however, I realized the true insanity was in many of the beliefs I'd held *before* everything blew to pieces. Through the challenging, exhausting, exciting process of unlearning, I began to realize that I wasn't who I'd believed myself to be. God wasn't what I thought God was. My past wasn't what I remembered, and no situation was only what I believed it to be at the time.

Even though I've pretty much always believed that we are spiritual beings having a human experience, I still had sold myself short my entire life. My programming convinced me that although I had talents and skills and could make a lot of things happen, I was, underneath it all, a small, separated being trying to make it through a challenging existence and do something positive with this one life I knew for sure I had. Because I had never fully questioned my basic assumptions or considered who I might be without the programming, I had been utterly blind to my true magnificence. Most of us are.

I described earlier the breakthrough experience in the little hot tub on that frigid morning when I became so profoundly aware of the present moment, lost track of my familiar sense of self, and even of the boundary around my physical body. There was a much deeper level to that experience that is difficult to put into words but I will do my best.

As my sense of personal boundary dissolved, I felt a brief flicker of fear that if I let go I wouldn't be able to make it back to myself, a flash of terror that maybe I was losing my hold on sanity. But almost instantly the fear was washed away by the deepest, most profound peace I'd ever experienced. I melted into a vastness, a connection, a oneness with a limitless, expansive Source presence. It was as though I was directly plugged into all of life, all of creation. I was swimming through, immersed in, and one with love in its purest form. I had never before felt so whole, so absolutely not alone. I knew in that instant that my being was far, far beyond anything I'd previously believed.

I didn't have the language at the time, but later realized this was my first conscious connection with the I Am, that part of us that is both us and the Creator and all of creation at once, that is simultaneously human and Divine being. This mystical experience was what *A Course in Miracles* calls the Holy Instant. In a Holy Instant we are completely in the present moment, free of the past and unconcerned with the future. It is a place of liberation and vast power and the place where we remember we are not little and alone. It is an experience of complete absence of fear and pure peace.

I didn't stay in that glorious place of a fully present, Holy Instant for long, but it stayed with me permanently. It was literally a life-changing moment. As my focus gradually shifted back to my body and I once again felt boundaries between me and the vastness, there was a small sadness and sense of loss, but I knew the connection wasn't forever lost and that I had been forever changed. From that moment forward I would experience life at a different level.

I still struggled, whipping back and forth for months between two primary states of consciousness. At times, most of the time actually, my mind was like a raging, thrashing wild beast, ripping and tearing around in fear and hatred, flinching away from the humiliation, guilt, and shame. But in spaces between, a stillness would break through and I would, once again, experience the utter calm and peace of becoming deeply present and sensing myself as connected with the vastness of creation and the Creator itself. It was as though the crack that had opened into a new awareness that cold winter morning in the ice and steam had not completely resealed and every so often something moved up through the fissure and took loving hold of my mind. I didn't know it then, but I was taking the first steps on a path toward re-membering, gathering up pieces of my True Self I had lost or forgotten, pulling my members back together.

As wildly uncomfortable as it is, loosing our grip on long-held beliefs, questioning what we think we know about ourselves and the world, provides a gateway into profound opportunity. The lives of those of us who step through such gateways will never be the same again—and we wouldn't want them to be.

Until we unlearn what we believe ourselves to be, we are accepting that we are nothing more than the personality we have created and the body we use to navigate through this world. Since we know those things are imperfect we are left with a deep sense of inadequacy and vulnerability. We fight so hard to protect our sense of identity, this ego we have created, not realizing we are fighting to preserve an illusion that is not even a shadow of our true, magnificent selves. Eckert Tolle calls ego identification, "A monstrous act of reductionism." We do terrible self-harm when we choose to identify this way.

This sense of inadequacy and imperfection is what drives the multibillion- dollar self-help industry. We work to fix the flawed or faulty aspects of ourselves. We strive to become better and more and different when the only thing that's really necessary is to truly remember or recognize who we already are. We do not improve ourselves or our world by rejecting what we are, or becoming something else, but by uncovering the glorious truth of our essential Selves. This rediscovery is the ultimate homecoming.

Our souls, our essences, long for awakening and evolution. I don't know if we somehow create or set up our dark night of the soul experiences but I do know they are portals through which we can act on the longing to return to Truth, to remember our oneness and wholeness. Those experiences that crucify the old, familiar self-identity always present opportunities for resurrection, renewal, and rebirth.

The purpose of the liminal phase in rite of passage rituals is to shake people's psyche loose from old moorings so that they can explore uncharted aspects of themselves, their community, and this miraculous, challenging gift of human existence. Each time we decide to question our own assumptions and genuinely consider whether we truly believe what we think we believe, we give ourselves a chance to grow, expand, and move to new places in life and work. Transformation begins when we open up to unlearning what we think we know.

One of the most powerful questions we can ask is, "*Who am I, really, underneath the layers of programming, and are my beliefs based in truth?*" In doing so we can scrub away old, useless, confining stories and beliefs, just like a snake rubs itself in the sand to shed the old skin that has grown small and worn.

One of my favorite passages in the *Course* advises:

Simply do this: Be still, and lay aside all thoughts of what you are and what God is; all concepts you have learned about the world; all images you hold about yourself. Empty your mind of everything it thinks is either true or false, good or bad, of every thought it judges worthy, and all the ideas of which it is ashamed. Hold onto nothing. Do not bring one thought the past has taught, nor one belief you ever learned before from anything. Forget this world, forget this course, and come with wholly empty hands unto your God.

I now believe something as catastrophic as my public shaming experience was necessary for me to begin to remove shackles I hadn't even realized I was wearing; I was just too strongly ego-identified to be able to break free without first being broken down. What a terrible shame it would have been had the breaking never occurred, had I never had the chance to begin to see who I truly am and who we all are.

Many people talk about finding God during very difficult circumstances and in times of great pain and need. In my case, I didn't find God; I found my Self, and in the process redefined God. I was given the gift of seeing that beneath the craziness of day-to-day life in this unhealthy world is a beauty and power that every soul aches for whether we're awake to the longing or not.

Opening up to deeply questioning everything we think we know, to unlearning some of the programming that has shaped our viewpoints and beliefs, is a fundamental key to unlocking the more that we are, and the wondrous, gorgeous more that life is. It might not be easy, but breaking down in order to break open to who we truly are is a s/hero's journey not to be missed. Through all of it, the letting go, the going deeper, we spiral a little higher and open up to an expansion of life and love.

CHAPTER 11

Regaining Consciousness

"What we are today comes from our thoughts of yesterday, and our present thoughts build our life of tomorrow: Our life is the creation of our mind."

—*Buddha*

The realization that we are not the personalities we think we are is a foundation-rocking discovery, one of those doors of knowledge that once opened can never be closed again. It's scary because we sense that we will have to give up a great deal if we release our old sense of self. There's a fear that maybe there will be nothing left to replace it and that we won't be able to function in the world without the identity we created for that very purpose. What I am learning is that this release requires no sacrifice, and in fact, coming to know that we are not small, weak, and alone is the greatest gift we can receive in this lifetime.

Who Do You Think You Are?

After the life-changing moment of awakening on that cold winter morning, I returned to the I Am consciousness over and over again. Each time, I experienced myself as vast, limitless, and powerful. I sensed oneness with Source, with the Divine energy behind all of creation. The more I did, the more I became aware of the Mind that was my actual being. I would notice myself thinking certain thoughts and then realize there was obviously an aspect of me that was not just the one having the thoughts, but rather the one *observing* the thinking. The more I focused on the observer, the more powerful and expansive I felt. Releasing my death grip attachment to the ego identity I'd believed myself to be allowed for the expansion into conscious awareness of the Me beyond body. At that level I could sense a vast potential that was just out of sight, not quite materialized. I was literally sensing a whole new layer and level of life and reality.

Over the next several very challenging yet transformative years, I immersed myself in spiritual study and even, despite early reservations, opened up to the teachings of Jesus that I had intentionally moved away from years earlier. From my new perspective and position I began to understand the difference between the religion *about* Jesus and the religion *of* Jesus. Unlike what I was taught as a child, Jesus wasn't saying, "Hey, follow me because my way is the only way—It's my way or the highway." Instead I believe Jesus was someone who had fully tapped into his innate divinity and had found a way of remembering who he truly was. As he shed the straitjacket of ego, he uncovered his true magnitude and magnificence and set out to show the rest of us how to do the same.

Relearning, reframing, and reclaiming Jesus' story and teachings was another tumbler clinking into place. Instead of just flat out rejecting all things from my early Christian exposure, as I'd done my entire adult life, I was now able to draw the tremendous wisdom of this master teacher into my diverse and eclectic spiritual base and add these profound teachings to that of other avatars and way-showers such as Buddha, Krishna, Native American wisdom teachers, and sages from across the ages.

That powerful mystical experience I had in the little hot tub that morning was my version of the "being born anew" that Jesus said a person had to go through in order to see the Kingdom of Heaven, a kingdom that is not some magical land in the clouds but a place, a space, a state of being that lies within each of us. During moments of being fully present, with no thought of future or past, we touch heaven.

In *Discover the Power Within You*, Eric Butterworth offers some profound insights into Jesus' unique concept of humanity and God. He writes, "When you come to yourself, when you wake up, when suddenly you come alive to the within of you, then God is very real to you—not as a person separate from you, but as an added dimension of you, as a living presence ever with you." This, I believe, is exactly what Jesus demonstrated. He was a human being who remembered his true identity and activated his innate divinity. He was able to live fully, full-time in Christ consciousness, a state of being that engages at the spiritual rather than purely physical level.

I now view Christ as not so much a religious term but rather a spiritual and even psychological one; it is a state of being and a way of thinking. It certainly is *not* Jesus' last name! Accepting Christ is not reaching out to some being beyond yourself, but instead opening up to the Christ consciousness that is innate in each of us. It is a coming home to the power we truly are. Marianne Williamson noted in her phenomenal book, *A Return to Love*, "Accepting the Christ is merely a shift in self-perception. We awaken from the dream that we are finite, isolated creatures, and recognize that we are glorious, infinitely creative spirits."

We are not just bodies. We are not just personalities. We are extensions of Divine Mind. It may seem audacious to consider oneself Divine, but for most of us it actually requires a massive act of humility to admit we were totally clueless about who we really were throughout our whole life up to that point! All the self-assurance, all the thinking we knew what we were doing was basically bumbling about blindfolded while ego, our little self, fed us BS about knowing what was in our best interest.

A Course in Miracles explains, "A concept of the self is made by you. It bears no likeness to yourself at all. It is an idol made to take the place of your reality ..."

We are expressions and extensions of God, like waves on the ocean, each unique, but also part of the whole. We are each divinity individualized, a cell in the collective consciousness. The more we open up to this self-identity, the better will be our lives and the more good we will bring into our world. Linda Martella-Whitsett, in *Divine Audacity*, notes, "Being the light requires us to claim, audaciously, our Divine Identity or I Am power. In an elevated awareness we understand that the source of the light is not personal, that I Am is not personal power. It is *spiritual* power."

I used to think that we were spiritual beings inside a body for a time. As I learn more about the power of Mind and how much our experience of reality is shaped by our perceptions and way of thinking, my view is shifting. I believe the relationship between our essence and our physical body is more like a virtual reality game. The body is a character created, projected, and maneuvered by the mind operating the controls. It's at the level of mind, becoming more conscious of what we actually are, that life gets really interesting and a whole lot more fun.

God as Matrix

Hand in hand with unlearning who I believed myself to be, I entered into a process of unlearning God. At the outset of my dark night transformation I hadn't even liked using the word God because it was too cluttered with the old connotations of a pretty unpleasant "out there" deity. In my twenties and thirties I had opened up to other spiritual paths and practices and my view of what God might be became more inclusive, more of a Mother-Earth-type creative spiritual force. I believed I'd moved past the notion of the "big guy in the sky" passing judgment. However, with the breaking of my life and ego I realized that no matter the face I was giving it, I was still viewing God as an entity, some sort of superbeing that was somewhere apart from me. I was still firmly in the fear-filled grip of the illusion of separation from Creator. The moment I began to question that old, programmed belief, my view of reality started to transform and a subtle, thrilling, yet nebulous sense of potential became a backdrop for most of my waking moments.

As I have more direct I Am, Holy Instant experiences, my sense of God as a personified being is falling away, being replaced by the sense of an energetic source, a field of power that all creation—matter and thoughts—arises out of. It's an all-encompassing energetic field, more like the Force in *Star Wars* than the God of conventional Christianity.

I've always felt like I could see behind certain veils. I could see some of the dark, sad truth, the wounds, insecurities, and hurts behind my father's horrific behavior. I became a professional new economy advocate and consultant because I could see the fundamental insanity of an economic model that destroys lives and the planet upon which it depends. Glimpsing behind the veil of the concept of God I was programmed with leads me to sense that God is something akin to the Matrix (from the movie so named) but in a good way. God is the fundamental everything that supports all things. It is the creative Divine Mind and the life substance that makes up all energy and form. God is Source and it is under, around, within, and through us. We emerged from it as an idea and then as form and therefore, we *are* it, at least as an extension or fractal of the whole.

I firmly believe that at the level of mind, which is what we actually are, we can directly interact with this Matrix, this Source that is God. That possibility is the sense of excitement and potential I feel coursing through everything, just out of sight, elusive but ever-present.

I was taught that God created mankind in his likeness. In reality, it's much more likely that we have created God in *our* likeness, because such an image is something we can get our minds around. However, it is also horrifically limiting and destructive. We all want to feel safe, but at a deep level very few actually do because we are buying into the illusion that we are small, weak beings, separated from one another and from the Creator. This single belief is the root of all our despair, dysfunction, and the damage we do to ourselves, one another, and our world. Doing the inner work to drop the literal death hold of that particular illusion is one of the greatest gifts we can give ourselves and everybody else.

We are in the likeness of God not through our physical forms but through the creative, generative power of our essential Selves, which is Mind and Spirit. As I first began to open up to this vastly different way of conceptualizing God it rattled me a bit because it seemed cold and impersonal. My experience, however, has proved just the opposite. This, I think, is why mystics and sages over the ages have defined God as love. In truth, I don't really know what "God is love" means, but I do know that when I am fully in the present moment, when I am having a Holy Instant experience, when I sense a direct connection to the vastness, I feel fully loved and loving at a level that far exceeds the typical experience of love between two human beings.

When I am acting based more on my Christ consciousness than ego, I act far more lovingly. This is Love as a creative, transcendent power. Often, if we allow it, intense hardships and trauma can transform our way of loving, broadening and deepening it and even allowing it to expand to people and creatures we might not have considered before. Allowing the current of love to flow through and from us always attracts more love to us.

When I first wrote this chapter I had it broken into subsections—"Who are You?" and "What is God?"—but realized that framing and language was just perpetuating the damaging false divide. We are in fact individualized extensions of God; God is experiencing creation through us. We are God expressing and the more we tune into that connectedness, the more love we have for others and ourselves.

As pieces of Godness, like waves on the ocean, each with a unique shape but still part of the ocean itself, we are simultaneously one with all and unique. *A Course in Miracles* describes the Holy Spirit as that part of us that remembers our oneness with God, Source, the Creator. A new habit I've picked up when meditating or praying is to focus on the "Big HS," meaning Holy Spirit and Highest Self. This helps reinforce a sense of at-one-ment with all that is and reminds us that prayer isn't about changing God's mind, but about shifting our own. It's not about begging some God out there somewhere, but about getting aligned with the Source energy from which we were created and through which we create.

Descartes had it backwards when he famously said, "I think, therefore I am." It is more, "I am, therefore I think." Yes, we wear bodies, and yes, we have brains, but it is the mind, that invisible, hard-to-define mystery, that holds consciousness, our awareness of existing, and all the perceptions that shape our view of the world and ourselves. Our bodies give us many great experiences but the real power is in our infinite and boundless minds.

Buddha noted that our lives are the creation of our minds. At the deepest level this may mean we are actually bringing into physical form that which we are conjuring and creating, good or bad, in our minds. At the very least the perspective we choose to take on any person, any thing, and any situation absolutely creates our experience of those people and events. It is at the level of consciousness that we choose, knowingly or not, how we view everything we experience. We believe the things and events we experience cause us to think and feel certain ways, but in fact it's just as true that how we think and the stories we tell ourselves dramatically shapes our experience of, and feelings about, events and interactions.

Consciousness, thoughts, and stories function like a self-reduction funnel. In order to expand, it is essential to learn to identify the stories we are telling ourselves and telling about ourselves and to increase our ability to notice our thoughts. As we gain skill in making those identifications and observations and take on the transformative exercise of telling different stories and learning to think different thoughts, we create opportunities for tremendous expansion. Each time we draw our minds away from the past or the future and dial in to our essence, our consciousness, we connect with the vastness that is our truth. We re-member with the Source, the wholeness of what we truly are. Oliver Wendell Holmes noted, "A mind that is stretched by a new experience can never go back to its old dimensions."

It is our mind, and the thoughts it produces and the feelings that result from those thoughts, that makes our life. The greatest goal and journey of our human experience is learning to gain control of our mind and its line of thinking. The key is remembering we do have the power to decide where we are going to throw the weight of our consciousness.

We are spiritual beings having a human experience as part of the evolutionary process of remembering the magnitude of who and what we truly are. As evolving spirits on a sacred spiral journey, every single situation is a classroom, and intense challenge is one of the very best classrooms for learning the life-changing discipline of taking control of our thoughts and rewriting our stories and coming to know we are not just at the mercy of events happening to us. This understanding enables limitations to be chipped away, revealing the awesome cathedrals of our True Selves.

CHAPTER 12

On Purpose

"Anything and everything you have experienced has been purposeful; it has brought you to where you are now."

—Iyanla Vanzant

I don't know if everything happens for a purpose, but I do know we can find purpose in everything that happens. Pulling value out of agony helps us make sense of traumatic events and is a powerful survival skill; it's also the thing that allows us to become more than we were before.

The greatest gift we can give ourselves and our world is to allow the trauma to break us open to the truth of who we really are, but be prepared: that opening process can send disruptive ripples throughout every aspect of your life. Once we've experienced the peace and power of the I Am consciousness, the connection to Source, once we've really laid hold of the fact that we're more than just these human bodies, our purpose and priorities often shift.

I've always wanted my life to matter, to serve a higher purpose. I believe my career in environmental and social change to be a calling, a noble, altruistic mission to make a positive contribution. I deeply love this small blue planet and all the creatures she supports. I wanted to play a big role in helping her heal and I still do. However, by the time the legal challenges and media coverage finally began to slowly wrap up, and I was able to focus on my career again, I realized I no longer wanted to do exactly what I was doing before. My core values hadn't shifted. I still loved the earth, nature, and the miraculous diversity of species we share her with, and I still wanted to make big, positive contributions, helping to heal and protect those things. My *what* was still intact, but my *how* had shifted enormously.

Einstein once noted, "We cannot solve our problems with the same level of thinking that created them." As good as my intentions had been in my career up to that point, my unexamined thinking and unrecognized ego identification had in fact been perpetuating the very problems I was working to solve. I was drawn to the political arena in part because I believed I could have a positive influence there but also because I liked the battle mentality, the competitiveness, and the "sport" of it.

It still feels like profound timing that I went through my politically motivated takedown and years of legal challenges and expenses during a time that the behavior being displayed in the US White House was egregiously egomaniacal, damaging, and divisive. Witnessing the massive and rapid erosion of civility and effectiveness in governance and the seeming inability to hold the perpetrators accountable while I was being disempowered and discarded due to false allegations left me disillusioned about our system of governance, politics, and media.

As I gained distance and perspective, and as I learned more about the psychology of ego versus authentic self, I came to see the whole arena I had been caught in was a devastating dance of egos. Reporters concocting stories and falsifying information in order to bring down people in higher positions than they. Politicians jockeying for the next position in ascension regardless of the fact they had no plan or ability to exercise leadership for the common good from the coveted position. Ethics officials pontificating and dragging out expensive proceedings in order to get a shot at a soundbite on the news that might make them appear important. And me, caught in the illusion of power and the desire to feel valuable and significant from the outside in.

Seeing myself attracted to what was a microcosm of the massive dysfunction being clearly displayed at the level of federal politics in the US caused me to question very deeply whether it was even possible to effect real and positive change through that arena. This was hard to face given that I had spent so many years in political endeavors. I didn't know what it would mean for my work and involvement going forward, but I did know that midway through my dark night of the soul I had already changed too much to go back to the frenetic, egoic activities, institutions, and groups that had been

so important to me before. I had new priorities and new gifts
to give. I also had shifting ideas about success.

I still want to be a successful influencer in the healing
of our planet and a successful business owner and author, but
there is now a deeper layer, a different priority that under-
pins it all. Success for me means that as I'm doing my best
work on every project before me I stay more and more in the
now moment, focused on all the things deserving my gratitude, and interacting kindly and lovingly with every being
I encounter. Success means working my tail off to make our
world a healthier, kinder place while also continuing to grow
and evolve as a spiritual entity. I now know that just being a
Human Doing isn't success. Success is in evolving as a Being
while in the process of the doing.

Prior to my big ordeal, because ego had been in the
driver's seat, I didn't view my own being, my kindnesses, the
simple love I gave to others, as genuinely important. My experience of being humbled and losing my position and platform
was publicly portrayed as a fall from grace; in reality it was a
fall into grace.

I came to understand that as much as I wanted to have
a big impact on big issues, my greatest contribution might be
the genuine conversation I have with the young man ring-
ing up my purchases at the grocery store or the older woman
serving me lunch at a local café. I came out the other side of
my humbling much more open, present, and willing to take
time for such small but beautiful encounters.

Over time, through the empowerment coaching and
ministry work, my mess has become my message. And being
a living demonstration of survival, resilience, transformation,

and reinvention is proving helpful to others. As I neared completion of all the legal complications that had been thrown at me, I got the biggest opportunity of my life to make a direct contribution; at long, long last, I picked my nephew up from prison.

Early on a cold morning in January 2019, I drove the rental car from a frigid little motel room across a whole lot of flat barrenness in northwest Oklahoma. I stopped at a gas station for a cup of coffee and, a mile and a half later, drove onto the prison grounds, comprised of razor-wire fences, guard towers, and bleakness. The full story and horror of a prison experience and the US system of so-called corrections will be the subject of another book, but the nutshell version may be useful to anyone seeking peace, power, and purpose while dealing with transition and reinvention.

Waiting there in the bleak prison office and reception area, I was very nervous. Jonathan had been in for ten years and I really did not know how he was going to react. Even more worrisome was that I wasn't sure the prison system was really going to allow his release. Over the years, his release date had been extended three times due to what were described as "auditing errors" and I had had to fight for nine months after he became eligible for a lower security level for them to finally transfer him out of the max facility, which happened to be a for-profit, privately run prison, in the business of making money on the inmates there.

The hour and a half I waited in the prison lobby now seems surreal. Finally, dressed in the black sweats and sweatshirt I had brought in that morning, my nephew emerged accompanied by a guard. I stood up to give him a hug and all six foot two inches and two hundred pounds of him collapsed sobbing in my arms. I didn't think he'd do that in front of the guards. He didn't think so either. As we turned to go, they handed him his only possessions—a box of all the correspondence he'd ever received, most of it from me. They handed me a blue folder containing his release paperwork. On the front was written his name and under that "Discharged to the street."

That is the fate of far, far too many people who wind up in the US prison system. They will be released to the street, without an aunt Cylvia there to pick them up, facing something like a mile and a half of partial dirt road leading to the nearest convenience store.

Watching Jonathan adjust to being in a car, going into a department store, accidentally locking himself out of the motel room (multiple times), trying to figure out the cell phone I'd brought him was heartbreaking and beautiful. It took a full five days to get his state ID and get on a plane back to Oregon.

John met us at the airport and the next day we headed over the mountains to my little home in Bend. Observing, supporting, and living with my nephew's reinvention and reentry is one of the hardest and richest experiences of my life. Despite his tremendously challenging past, and the PTSD from the cumulative experiences of childhood trauma and prison, within three weeks he had a full-time job. Within two months he was able to get a driver's license and I had the gift wrapped in barbed wire of teaching a young person how to drive using my only car! A few weeks after that he had saved enough to buy a car and two days after that, he landed a second job. His struggles are massive, but so far his motivation and work ethic is equal to the task.

For someone who has faced my own reentry and reinvention and is now in the business of helping others do the same, there could be no richer classroom or more profound inspiration than having my nephew live with me as he navigated this stage of his life. In the grand scheme of things, was this the reason I chose, so early in life, not to have children? Was this the reason I was put on the path of transition and empowerment coaching? I don't know, but I do know that I can choose for this experience to add more purpose and meaning to those events in my own life. Although, like so many parents I feel as though I'm screwing up left and right, I also know I have far, far more skills and patience than I would have had without the challenging experiences of the past many years and the growth and training I stepped into as part of my own reinvention process. And I know I wouldn't be as empathetic, as loving, as forgiving, or as mature (even though I have a long way to go in all those areas) had I not gone through my own humbling.

Jonathan knew some of the challenges I'd been dealing with and that opened his heart more fully to me as well. Was it all divinely laid out for a specific purpose? I don't know, but I do know there is purpose to be found in it.

The three years following the day my life blew up turned out to be the hardest, and the richest, of my life to that point. I believe they had a purpose and that purpose was to help me recognize who I really am and share what I've learned about trauma, transformation, and reinvention with others who are determined to harness their challenges to make their lives and our world healthier, saner, and more beautiful.

A Course in Miracles explains that until we understand that we are more than our personas, our egos, we allow our genuine free will to be imprisoned. The prisons that are the most difficult to escape are not those built with concrete, razor wire, and patrolled with guns but those we sentence ourselves to through our own beliefs, stories, and unchallenged programming, and only we hold the key to those cells.

Our greatest challenges and deepest wounds are usually the best catalysts to propel us forward on a pathway of growth and expansion. Our times of deep loss and uncertainty are the times to go within, not to hole up and shrink, but to whole up, expand, and get very clear about what we really want to do with this precious human life we've taken on.

I am in no way suggesting that the goal is all about focusing on the spiritual and ignoring or neglecting daily life, career, the goals and dreams we have for our life right here on this physical planet. Not at all! Developing awareness of our True Selves massively empowers our way of being in this world and it sure as heck makes our human experience a more peaceful, fun adventure.

As we move through our tough ordeals, if we choose to allow the trauma to break us open, we will have new gifts to give our world. That doesn't necessarily mean we abandon long-held life goals and ambitions, but we may very well want to go about them differently, and want to be different while in the midst of pursuing success in the doing.

I now believe that the most important purpose of these human lives is the journey back to Self and Truth, to remembering we are not just these human bodies and personalities. Our most important work is to expand our consciousness and open up to our full potential and power. Every single one of the challenges and traumas we face provides an opportunity to do exactly that. The point is never the crucifixion. And it's not about the ones jabbing spears or pounding the nails. The whole point is the resurrection, the incredible strength and beauty that rises up *because* of the challenge. We do ourselves, and our world, a terrible disservice when we waste the crises in our lives. What better way to transmute hardship than to expand into our True Selves and move forward through this world from a place of greater peace and power? That is the choice, the opportunity, and the responsibility before us and it is glorious.

CHAPTER 13

The Beginning

Four years, eight months, and thirteen days after my life blew up, all the legal and media challenges finally came to a close. The State of Oregon and Oregon DOJ had contested my bankruptcy agreement, seemingly wanting to force me into foreclosure. They failed. I was finally free to focus fully forward.

This is normally the point in a book where you'd find an epilogue but that doesn't seem fitting in a book about the journey of identity destruction, transformation, and reinvention. When life blows to pieces and we make it through the arduous ordeal of putting ourselves back together, there really is no conclusion. In birth, and rebirth, there are only beginnings.

Three weeks after the legal and media challenges ended, my beloved, beloved Tessa passed very quickly after an unexpected discovery of abdominal cancer. I was able to be with her twenty-four hours a day the last several days and keep her comfortable and pampered. She passed in our front room with her head in my lap. For many, our stickiest people don't necessarily come in human form and Tessa and John were my most steadfast and important. The pain of her passing was terrible, the deepest and most profound grief of my life, and yet, every bit worth it for the experience of her and our lives together.

Was there a purpose in the timing of her transition? I don't know. I do know had it come two years earlier I might not have survived it. When it did come, once the gutting, cutting grief lost its edge, the rawness of missing her put me in a softer, slower, more reflective space that helped me finish this book.

Throughout my long ordeal and the stretch of unresolved, prolonged challenges there were so many times I was desperate for it just to be over with so that I could move on with life. But now I see that a quick resolution would have been a terrible lost opportunity. My evolution required longer incubation; had the catastrophe resolved sooner, I would have been like a butterfly pulled prematurely from the chrysalis with wings too underdeveloped and deformed ever to fly. I can now see that the whole thing played out in beautiful Divine timing.

While nearing the end of all of the legal and media battles and, unbeknownst to me, the end of my time on Earth with Tessa, I had a powerful dream:

> *I am giving birth and I know the tiny infant is me. I am flooded with love for her and wrap her in a snuggly blanket. But then, I put her*

*down inside my large purse and lean it up
against the outside of a building. I go inside
and start working on some project with a
team of people. After a little while, I realize,
"Oh my God, I left the baby out in the cold!"*

*I rush out and find the bag with the infant
me in it. The little one is basically okay, but
very cold, and I hold her against my body,
giving her warmth and love. And then, I
put her back in the bag and go back inside
the building to work.*

*After a time, I once again remember I've
left her outside and in a panic, afraid I will
find her dead, I rush back out and pick her
up. I hold her close, rock her gently, and
promise never, ever to abandon her again.
I am flooded with love as the dream ends.*

I think we do some version of this over and over, when
we put aside our true glorious Selves and opt to be something
less than we really are. We do it when we change our true
nature to conform to someone else's idea of what we should
be. We do it when we compare ourselves to others and believe
we are coming up short or when we act with less integrity than
we know we are capable of. We do it when we beat ourselves
up for a simple human mistake and we do it every single time
we choose to believe we are small, powerless, and alone.

The day my life blew up I never could have imagined I
would become a minister and a certified life empowerment
coach. I never would have believed my first full book would

be about my long ordeal of public shaming, recovery, and reinvention or that I would create a program helping people in times of great transition launch the next awesome chapters of their lives. I would never have imagined I'd make a group of three dear, beloved women friends/sisters through the ongoing study of *A Course in Miracles,* and I couldn't have known how difficult or deeply beautiful it would be to have my nephew living with me as he launches his new life of freedom and health. I couldn't have foreseen the depths of compassion and love John and I would discover as we moved through the shared sorrow, struggle, uncertainty, and rebirth.

Incredibly, after all of this, despite all of this, in fact *because* of all of this, I am truly happier and more at peace than ever before. The relationships that matter are stronger. I now have regular moments of intense, empowered deep connection to Creation and Source, to the *me* beyond this body. My heart has opened and softened and beauty unfailingly appears where I'd been blind to it before. I love more deeply.

The truth is none of us really have any idea what's coming next despite our incessant planning. It makes me smile even as I make my next plans. Those include developing a program to help people transitioning out of incarceration get jobs and a fresh start by doing work that benefits our earth and teaching college courses on creating a saner, more sustainable economy. I'm planning my next big writing projects—a piece titled *"Released to the Street"* about Jonathan's experience of prison and mine of supporting him as he survived his sentence and then faced the incredible barriers that society puts in front of people trying to restart their lives on the other side of incarceration.

Thanks to Tessa's inspiration, I'm also planning a book titled, *Soul Dog*, for all of us who know the indescribable, profound, and life-changing experience of giving our whole hearts to our four-legged, furred, or feathered friends. And, sometime in the months to come, when my heart has healed, I plan to bring a new beloved canine friend into my life and home again.

Those are the plans for now, subject to change, as everything always is.

There is life before we meet, or at least brush up against, our True Selves, and life after. Once we open to the transformative experience of moving into a conscious awareness of the I Am, of our connection with all of creation and the exquisite peace that comes with it, we are never the same. No matter how much we may screw up, how many times we fall or fail, how many times we act from ego instead of Divine Self, the peace of that knowing is always there when we choose to go home to it.

I've heard it said a forest is not so much a thing as it is a process. Trees grow, stretch toward the sun, get struck by lightning or seared by wildfire. Even in death the trees support tremendous life, becoming home to myriad insects, fungi, and bacteria. New baby trees grow along and around them.

Our lives are like that too. Not so much a journey with a beginning point and end destination, but a process of growth, learning, unlearning, and awakening. Never static, ever amazing.

May we each open to the beauty and magic,
ever-present, even in the hard things.

May we find the strength to feel deeply and not duck away from the grief, the loss, the joy, the vastness of love.

May we always be brave enough to fail and bold enough to get up, patch up our scrapes, and get back in the game of living fully.

May we all be courageous enough to question everything we think we know, trusting that Truth is always eager to be found.

May each and every one of us remember who we truly are and share that magnificence with ourselves, one another, and our world.

Amen and onward ...

We are each far more than a job, a title, a financial status, a criminal background, a role. We are more than a body. We are more than we know, and we have a choice to make. We can fight to hold fast to the selves we think we are, or we can choose to let the death of the old and familiar give birth to our *True* Selves. Every single moment holds the opportunity of rebirth, no matter what is swirling in the outer circumstances of our lives just now. It's not the crucifixion that matters; it's the resurrection. Your Easter is here—if you choose it.

ACKNOWLEDGMENTS

This book took a long time to write, nearly five years in fact. Its creation mirrors the odyssey of my own healing and growth throughout the whole long affair. It's so clear now that the early drafts were attempts to exonerate myself, to point fingers at those who put the shaming in motion and those who piled on. I even had an eager agent on board for the early version of the book. Thank goodness no publishers picked it up! I was so far from being healed enough to put forward a book of any real value.

The book morphed many times after that, gradually shifting from political intrigue to memoir to personal development. Three different times I thought I had finished, only to have something or someone prompt me to realize it still wasn't right.

The big breakthrough came when I finally began to understand the story of what happened to me doesn't really matter. Although the ego me didn't like such a thought, the me that's something more knew it was the truth. The little me wanted people to know about and be appalled by the attacks and unfairness of it all, wanted people to know how awful the attackers were. My True Self knew that wasn't the point. What matters aren't the events that broke my life; what matters is what broke open inside and through me as a result.

So I open my acknowledgements with deep gratitude to Divine Guidance and to my Highest Self who stayed the course and maintained the patience and discipline to allow the book to become something I feel really good about offering our world.

Although I had incalculable help along the way, no one supported and encouraged me more than my beloved John, always encouraging me forward even while dealing with his own tremendous grief and loss. Dearest, you are my stickiest person of all and there simply is no adequate way to express my appreciation of and to you. As I've said many times before, I wish I could open that little door in my mind and heart and let you directly feel what I feel for you so that you could experience the full depth and beauty of who I see you to be. I love you beyond measure.

Jonathan, my unconventional son, you and I have a lot in common and in some ways understand one another like nobody else can. Having you live with me while you built your life of freedom and success was such a challenge. So many times I wanted to pull my hair out, or even better, yours, but the truth is I wouldn't have missed it for anything. Having you in my life, and in my home has added such incredible richness and love. Watching your journey is an inspiration and a joy. I am so proud I get to be your mama.

And Mother, I am so grateful we have become friends and grateful I allowed my perspective to shift so that I could get over myself and stale, old stories and see the beauty of you.

Thank you for your powerful example of strength, gratitude, and choosing happiness.

To my fleet of attorneys, who I affectionately and respectfully call my Dream Team, thank you, once again, for all the support. Though you didn't directly help in the writing of this book, I wouldn't have been in a position to do so without you.

The list of other friends and supporters who helped me during my long ordeal is too long to include in its entirety but I want to name some so that you know how much you mattered. Reverend Jane Hiatt, your love, presence, wisdom, and teaching was powerful therapy. Bruce Rinaldi, your wisdom, guidance, humor, and love was so unexpected and such a tremendous gift. Jason and Marla Jo Hardy, my "fiercely protective" neighbors and dear friends, I want you to know I now describe you as non-DNA family. Carole and Bob Tucker and Steve and Kathryn Gray, my non-DNA parents, the support you've provided over the past twenty years cannot be measured; I am so, so grateful for you. Jennifer, Marilyn, and Shera, our *Course in Miracles* journey has been such a tremendous gift as are the friendships that grew out of it.

Dick Withnell, Lee Larson, and John Nash, your generosity not only helped pay the bills when I didn't know how I was going to do so, but your willingness to invest in me at such a low and broken point in my life gave me a little boost toward remembering that I was indeed worth something.

No fewer than three dozen people helped directly with the completion of this book. Some read early drafts and gave me feedback, some helped pay the editing and publishing costs—all of you are deeply appreciated. Michael Davis, you went above and beyond with your generous editing advice as well as your fierce support.

I want to thank all the authors and teachers who inspired, educated, and enlightened as I moved forward on my journey of healing and awakening. And thank you to all the strangers who stepped forward with kindness; you will never know the difference you made.

Beloved Tessa dog, I still feel your presence so strongly and miss you intensely. You never earned a fancy vest but you certainly were my therapy dog. Wherever you are now, may you know that I still think of you and say as I did so many times, "Do you know how much I love you?" and I smile in response to your smile.

Finally, I give thanks to and for the attackers, opponents, and fearful people. The stones you hurled broke through my house of glass. Over time, that gift wrapped in barbed wire surmounted and subdued my stubbornness, ego, and misplaced will, giving me a chance to touch beauty I never imagined.

I am deeply thankful for ongoing rebirth.

RESOURCES AND RECOMMENDED READING

The Book of Awakening by Mark Nepo

The Book of Forgiving by Desmond and Mpho Tutu

A Course in Miracles published by Foundation for Inner Peace

Conscious Living: Finding Joy in the Real World by Gay Hendricks.

Discover the Power Within You by Eric Butterworth

Emotional Chaos to Clarity by Phillip Moffit

In the Flow of Life by Eric Butterworth

Lessons in Truth by H. Emilie Cady

A New Earth by Eckhart Tolle

The Places that Scare You by Pema Chodron

The Power of Now by Eckhart Tolle

A Return to Love by Marianne Williamson

Rising Strong by Brené Brown.

Untethered Soul by Michael Singer

When Everything Changes, Change Everything by Neale Donald Walsh

www.CylviaHayes.Com
www.facebook.com/cylviahayespublic/

ABOUT THE AUTHOR

Cylvia Hayes is an award-winning public speaker, empowerment coach, new economy strategist, and professional environmentalist. In 2014, while serving as First Lady of Oregon, Cylvia became the target of a devastating politically motivated public shaming that went on for several years. This led to a deep inner awakening that changed the course of her career, her life, and her concept of herself.

Cylvia's coaching work centers on helping people facing transition and reinvention. She is the founder and CEO of 3EStrategies, a long-standing social enterprise consulting firm and director of Anew, a project that supports people transitioning out of incarceration and into jobs in environmental, renewable energy, and sustainability sectors. Cylvia is developing a college-level course on Economic Illusions, Truths, and Dangerous Assumptions. To her amazement and amusement, she is well into the training to become an ordained Unity minister.

Cylvia lives in Bend, Oregon, with a home and backyard like a wildlife sanctuary. Her greatest loves are her life partner, John; her son, Jonathan; dogs; horses; hiking and camping; and all things nature.

For more information, visit:
www.CylviaHayes.com and
www.3estrategies.org.

Made in the USA
Middletown, DE
21 February 2020